THE BORDERLINE DIARIES

THE
BORDERLINE
DIARIES

Elisa Frank
for Kimberley

A record of this publication is available from the British Library.

ISBN 978-1-910027-01-1

Typesetting by Wordzworth Ltd
www.wordzworth.com

Cover design by Titanium Design Ltd
www.titaniumdesign.co.uk

Printed by Lightning Source UK
www.lightningsource.com

Cover image by the author

Published by Local Legend
www.local-legend.co.uk

ABOUT THE AUTHOR

As a troubled teenager, Elisa Frank was groomed in her home town of Wakefield, Yorkshire, by an apparently charming asylum-seeker, Ahmad Otak, from Afghanistan. But his behaviour became more and more extreme and controlling until at last, in 2012, Elisa gathered the courage to flee to her sister's home. Otak followed and, making a pretence of sorrow, was allowed inside.

He then violently murdered Kim Frank, who was seventeen, with a knife while forcing a restrained Elisa to watch. When the girls' friend Samantha Sykes arrived, she suffered the same fate. Otak abducted Elisa and fled by car to Dover in an attempt to leave the country, but was arrested there.

Otak is serving a life sentence in prison. But Elisa is also suffering her own life sentence, utterly devastated by these events and the abject grief of losing her sister, with whom she had been very close. She spent several months in a psychiatric hospital, with Post Traumatic Stress Disorder and a Borderline Personality Disorder. Hence the title of this book.

In this book, Elisa does not dwell on the tragedy save to tell us what happened before her eyes and show us how it affected her mind. Then, with great courage, she describes how she began to heal. Her observation of both others' behaviour around her and of her own inner states is at times breathtaking, and always humbling.

We should all learn much from this perceptive, talented and brave young woman. Elisa still lives in Wakefield and is determined to honour her sister's and friend's memories by succeeding as a writer.

DEDICATION

This book is dedicated to Kimberley Louise Frank, my darling sister. "Me and you, twins for life, remember!" You may not be breathing the same way as I am, but our bond breaks through the veil of death. I hope you are proud of me and I'm sorry that I never used to tell you that I love you, and I always will.

I also dedicate my writing to Samantha Sykes, a much-loved friend who will be in many people's hearts forever. I wish that, in time, all of those heavily affected by grief, anger and loss will find some way to heal the pain and find peace through the spirits of the two girls, Kim and Sammy, who live on in spirit and in memory.

ACKNOWLEDGEMENTS

Firstly, it is important to thank Kim for keeping my spirit alive throughout my writing and spurring me on to share this with the world. And I would like to thank all my family for being there for me during these years. Mum and Faye, you are the best and I love you. I give many thanks to my father for always believing in me, for keeping me inspired and smiling during the long hours when I thought I could not make it; here is our future, Dad, writing as we always said we would. Thanks to David Stephens for helping me in every way he can; he is a star.

Thank you to my friends who have been neglected during this period of creating my story: Natalie Catchpole, Dean Hancock, my online friends and Kim's friends and the many others I've met on the way. Thank you to all those with whom I spent time in Fieldhead Hospital; those small things you all did and said brightened my world and made a real difference. And thanks to my fictional character Mel, too; we have ticked off the first thing on the bucket list.

A big thank-you too to my Connexions worker, Keiley Habron, for your advice through thick and thin and for giving me hope of a future for myself when there seemed to be none. You are a wise owl and I often think of what you might say in the hours when I need advice.

Finally, of course, I thank my publisher Nigel Peace for his help in putting this book together and giving me a chance to share my work with all of you.

CONTENTS

PROLOGUE:
THE DOLLS

She was still and doll-like... a porcelain doll... her ragdoll sister stared down at her as if in an out-of-body experience... I was the ragdoll, Elisa. But please call me Lacey as this is my alter ego. I had only just turned into a real and tangible being after leaving an evil man who'd dressed me only in black and blue. He'd seen me as a ragdoll.

The porcelain one was Kim and she wasn't always a doll. In fact she never was until her insides gave in, until she endured this deadly attack, several blows with a nine-inch knife to her torso, the final one to her jugular. That rendered her into a transition, the one where the spirit leaves the vessel and changes itself into something else, something beautiful, something doll-like. But this transition was not beautiful. It was tragic in every sense, it was painful and horrific and done to her in the name of love by a narcissistic brute with no heart who wanted to keep me prisoner. He saw my sister as an obstacle.

I had never wanted this man but he'd sucked me in with fineries and delicacies, sweet like mango, which he used to force-feed me with, feigning admiration. I'd been in a bad way, a depressive state with nowhere to live at the time when I made the decision to accept his hand. My world was empty until, gradually and perilously, I gave myself up to his ownership. Before I knew it I was bound and chained to the house of horrors where we lived together.

Then I'd escaped, as frightened as one could ever be, and I was in a frozen state that day, the day that was the end of everything. He came around and tricked his way into our 'candy house', Kim's flat, where we two sisters sat sipping tea, eating Rich Tea biscuits and planning future double dates. When the bell sounded we let him in thinking that he was coming to bring my kitten. Although I loved my kitten a lot, I'd left him behind in the house of horrors when I fled. Since then I'd been scared that the kitten would have the fate Otak had often joked about, which was to crucify him.

He entered, with a deadly intent that neither of us picked up on, and simply asked for a drink of water. I gave him one and he handed Kim a cigarette, making jokes which she seemed to find amusing. But I didn't want even to see this man who had violated me endlessly in the year I had spent as his secluded prisoner. I told him to leave and said I'd talk to him later, which was a lie. And that was that. We led him to the doorway.

But we didn't quite make it…

I felt my sister shove into me, turned around and saw the kitchen knife, shiny, deadly. Then everything was just a flash of images… blood splattered on pastel walls, my sister shrieked "Elisa!" I was on the floor and Otak had his grip around my upper arm as I tried to reach for the door, trying so hard, not for my own life but for my sister, whose screams were of pure horror. Unless you've witnessed great violence, you are blessed never to have heard such screams, high-pitched and piercing, screeching out in pain and blood-curdling.

Somehow we ended up in the living room… how? The front door was near the bedroom, closer than close and yet I failed for the handle, I really failed, I failed in every sense that one could. I could see all around the living room setting and I looked at myself, knowing that I had not been injured physically. But then

I looked around at my sister who was wrenching over as Otak like an animal made arm thrusts with the knife, with great force.

I tried to calm my nerves, telling myself that I was going to be next. When you're presented with a situation like this, survival is all you think of... if you think of anything at all.

Kim received a hard blow to the throat. The final blow. Somehow, naively, I still thought she would stay alive. My sister was a no-nonsense kind of character, not a weak one, not one who dies... and I held onto this belief until she was on the floor, gurgling. Kim was leaving. And this is when it dawned on me, so slowly and tenderly, so bizarrely, that I was witnessing my beautiful sister helplessly dying. It was happening rapidly, her breaths becoming shallower by the second, until they simply ceased. Just like that.

Her body was a disgraceful mess. He had made her a disgrace when really she was a beautiful creature. And I wanted so badly to hold my sister's hand and tell her it would be okay. But Otak immediately tied me up and stood in front of me, licking the bloody knife and grinning.

The sisters' candy house melted around me into nothingness and my young sister's once smiley face, full of endless vitality, melted into a contorted sadness. But I had to live with the burden of not one death of the divine, but two. On that fateful day, Otak's hunger had not stopped at just the death of Kim, it had to take another loved one too, another one of life's treasures, my beautiful friend Samantha. She was the kind of girl everybody loved, my best friend since childhood. I was forced to make a call to her, as my sister lay bloody and broken, inviting her to come round. Inviting her into her own death. I didn't know she was going to die, I thought she would be able to help me - another example of our illusion that the young and happy will live forever. Even from those who are full of life and youth, life can be taken swiftly. She went the same way as Kim... she gurgled for a few minutes, then death set in and her eyes deadened. My soul then began to burn and the fire spread all through me and around me, leaving me in my own Hell, metaphorical and real, over the weeks that followed.

I lost my heart the day of the doll's burial. The funeral director had invited me to choose an outfit for her, so I chose jeans and a nice tee-shirt; my aunt suggested a scarf too, claiming it was a pretty scarf, but we all knew it was really to cover the neck lacerations. I visited the mortuary prior to this and felt my own punctured lungs collapse at the sight of the vessel before me... It was weird to see a body without a soul. Immensely surreal. I planted a kiss on my sister's cold, porcelain head. Nothing is as cold as death, nothing as heart-breaking as seeing the coffin of a young person lifted down, as time stands still, into the earth, as loved ones throw roses down with love.

SOAR WITH THE ANGELS

watch me Daddy
watch me fly
I'll soar with the angels
and fly through the sky
watch me fade out of this life
watch me wish my life away
take me from reality
let us leave the world today

Daddy tell me why so sad
Daddy tell me why you cry
your little girl no longer lives a lie

now I have let go
this is the end
there is no going back
but now I soar, fly through the sky
I'll fly to the stars and sit on a cloud
I am so high
I feel so proud
just remember in your heart
that when you're down
I'll sprinkle you with my love

(*Soar With the Angels* was written by Kim, four months before her death)

I've had such a hard time, dear Kim, and am still wondering why you're not around; but I know you have not left me, we would never leave each other. It's been a massive haze of heavy confusion for me over these past few days and I think I am suffering a mind sickness as my brain feels dead. You haven't died, you can't have. You are a strong person, invincible, nobody could ever hurt you. Listen... I need your advice, I need your help... please tell me what the fuck to do. I've wracked my brain attempting to figure out what you would say to me right now. And in a sick way I know I should thank you too, for helping me survive 'til this point. But where are you now? You shouldn't have gone. Why didn't you hang on? How can one of us survive without the other? It's absurd because there is now no way forward or backwards.

Your boyfriend called my 'phone many times. I said, "I don't know where she is." He sounded really upset.

If for argument's sake you are gone, then what will I do? I will wait for you to come back. Otak is behind bars so we can be together again, reunited like we always planned to be. Try to listen, please, you're the only one who understands me. Just tell me where the Hell you are. I cannot cope when you're not around, there's no life in me. Tell me, should I go on – living, I mean? Two girls have been murdered in Barden Road, stabbed to death, and I was there when it happened… I was there and I survived it… I don't know why. Maybe you think I am not making sense… maybe that's why you're not responding to me. I am aware I don't make sense.

Just come back please. Come back and I'll make it all better and for once in my life I will help someone else, you and Sammy. I need you here and I'll wrap Band Aids around your wounds, for they should have been mine. I know I have not been there for you over this past year. I know I have failed you as a sister and a best friend. I'm sorry for all those times you came round to the house of horrors and I didn't answer… I pretended there was nobody in… I know there's no excuse but he wouldn't let me answer to you, he was always jealous of you, he knew how much you meant to me and that Sammy was the only friend I have ever had.

I'll write again soon and I won't stop writing until you are returned to me. Promise me one thing? One day you will come back to me, but don't wait too long. I love you forever and always. Me and you… twins for life, right? Distance never kept us apart before.

Soulless and mute, my heart was burning up with desire just to say "Goodbye", but unlike the phoenix my heart did not begin a rebirth. It just sat in my chest weighed down with such heavy sadness, the whole sadness of the world, it felt. Then an angel above caught on to this, and was immediately and urgently sent by God to remove my heart and destroy it. It was taken from me by a messenger angel who burned it immediately upon returning to the Heavens. One could never live with such a heavy organ that mine had become, so initially this was a relief.

From there I denied the world for a while and withdrew completely, planning my suicide daily. The void, deep and inconsolable, was a curse. But even though I yearned for the grave, I just couldn't do it. I couldn't let the animal win.

My sister visited me in spirit form, I believe, telling me that I needed to fill my chest with a new heart; she would wrap it up in barbed wire so no-one could damage it again. I just needed to find a heart, for one cannot live with an empty chest any more than one can live with a heavy heart. So to gain a new heart, I began believing in love again. From each new lover that I found, I stole their heart to make it my own. But each time I realised they didn't fit well in my chest, and I couldn't bring myself to watch lovers go heartless for they became depressed so quickly. So I returned them to their rightful owners, when I left them high and dry.

I decided that no lover could be kind enough to give me their own heart for keeps and allow themselves empty suffering, yet still I clung on to the idea that maybe, one day, I would find this self-sacrificing person. But at the same time I knew that I would have to tell him or her that their heart was too kind and pure, so I couldn't take it after all. I could never win.

So I decided to create a character called Mel, short for Melancholy, and take his heart instead. Now, he had the heart of a poet, so when my sister's spirit had fitted barbed wire around this new heart, that beat sweetly in my newly stitched-up chest, now I decided to fulfil my sister's dreams for me... to become a writer.

FADING... DYING

You're fading...
fading in and out,
undeniably disappearing
in a fashion,
you're dying

Your lungs trying,
heart sighing silently,
inevitably disintegrating.
This is nonsense.
You're dying?

You're merging,
merging with the earth,
terrifyingly transitioning,
no longer in a state of
dying.

I am fading...
fading in and out,
silencing sadness.
Instantly blood gushes
and I am coming...
I am dying.

ONE

THE NYMPH OF THE AIR

The nymph of the air
had luminescent hair.
The nymph was a girl
but the girl was destroyed
by crippling sadness,
by an empty sickness.
The grieving nymph melted,
she melted mercilessly
into that sadness.
And with buttercup kisses
she kissed velvet skies
where her sister now lies.

I am a nymph dancing around the hospital bedroom and these walls cannot confine me. I wear my tartan tutu, Alice in Wonderland knee-high socks, and leopard-skin Doc Martens. I have been detained here for a week and I have recently been given - from an angel or something - the honour of becoming a banshee. Family Liaison officers detained me under the Mental Health Act from where I was living with my

1

aunt and uncle. I kicked and I screamed and I cried uncontrollably when they told me I was unwell and they were taking me to Fieldhead.

I told them over and over and over that I was not 'crazy' and I kept saying it but they looked completely unconvinced as I sat in the back of their car while they drove me to the looney bin. Well, what can I say? Sanity is a hard act to sustain. They told me that they thought I was mentally ill and I told them, "If you are basing suspected mental illness on my current behaviour then you're stupid, because I've always had odd behaviour - so have I therefore always been mentally ill?" I must admit I would not be shocked to find that 'grief' had been added to the DSM's newest edition. Hmm... 'adjustment disorder' was used to describe me a few weeks ago. To hell with psychiatry.

The Family Liaison officers' job is to help, and also to deal with how the family is coping after homicides and the like, usually concerning the trial - the conviction that we all wait for, although we know it is not really a punishment. These partners who are dealing with my case are very nice; the woman reminds me of Morticia Adams (in a good way) and the guy bought me some cigarettes to bring in here with me.

I am a banshee, under certain conditions, when the lights on the ward go out. Strict darkness seeps into my soul and all is silent until the Zopiclone takes me and allows me into alternative realities where I am everything and anything... But currently I am enjoying singing for the imminently doomed men that I find in the streets of my mind, which unfurl before me as soon as my head hits the pillow. I am enjoying having a nice singing voice. I am like a nightingale as I lure the poor souls into a euphoric tune, fooling them into thinking I am something close to beautiful. Their demise brings me pleasure, as a banshee.

How did this happen to me? Well, after my spiritual death (I cannot pinpoint the exact date of this, but I should guess around the 10th of March) I was reborn as a spiritually renewed and awakened individual. I quickly realised and understood that 'reality' is very much subjective; this implies that I can escape this world during dreams, so I began doing so. My nightmares have subsided since. The doctor told me upon arrival that I suffer from 'emotionally unstable personality disorder'; he suspected Post Traumatic Stress Disorder first, because that would be anybody's assumption after the event.

There have been interventions with the mental health services, obviously after I suffered trauma, but also long before the trauma ever took place, throughout my adolescence. The doctor presented his theory to me that the death of my sister had aggravated the personality disorder somewhat. My personality has always been very unconventional and apparently the way I am handling my grief is atypical. He said that my problems are "indeed complex" - but enough of that, I want to make believe for a while…

I am such a graceful dancer, ignoring the bruises from where I often bump into things; I could have been a ballerina in a past life, or a swan. I dance with melancholy and over this past week all the patients and staff have seen my dance! They watch me: the patients smile and the nurses frown, looking slightly perplexed. I know they are envious of such graceful skill. I can't stay still. I am at one with the hidden melody of nature… or something along those lines. I am moving in and out of realms and possibilities that never occurred to me before my trauma. I am in a waking dream, and it is bloody marvellous. Oh, the freedom! Now nobody dictates my behaviour, they don't mind control me, I am free in thought and action.

I can smile without receiving a smack in the mouth.

Earlier, I made friends with a strange girl whom I decided was a lesbian after she offered me flowers. She had picked bright daffodils from the hospital grounds; at the time I didn't realise this was a platonic greeting that happens amongst patients here frequently. She asked me if she could dance with me. I was dancing to The Smiths, in one of the lounges.

"You are such a good dancer," she said. I noted that her eyes looked rather wild and grey in colour, her accent was odd and her words had to be listened to closely to comprehend. I was dancing to There Is A Light And It Never Goes Out and the lyrics seemed very apt to me. Morrissey's voice resonated within me and spoke to my soul.

"Thanks," I replied and we danced together. Just the two of us… until an idea hit me. "Hey, I can pole dance," I said gleefully.

She gasped, "Really? Wow."

"Yeah, I took, like, three pole dancing classes not so long back," I replied, feeling rather damn good about myself. "Wanna see?" I said, grabbing her loose hand from by her side, then racing into the main lounge where a good number of patients and fatigued-looking staff were seated watching TV. I jumped up onto the beam in the centre of the room and, although it was too wide, attempted to swirl around it.

"Get down, Elisa!" the staff shouted as though offended by this.

Some laid-back patients laughed and some looked indifferent. I just laughed too, then danced off back into the other lounge with the daffodil girl. We spent more time dancing and every hour the staff checked on us, looking at me with a funny expression. I know now that they are evidently envious. Obviously they all have two left feet. I dance around constantly now; life is a tricky dance to perform, but my movements are easy and I do not struggle. I also love music now in a different way to how I did before. I used to listen, sing along occasionally, but I didn't really listen and feel. Now I do not just listen but I become a part of the song. And every emotion I feel now is heightened and so real that I actually feel it with my new melancholic heart.

As I exit for a cigarette and a quick breather, I see Adam, a patient whom I met in the medication queue within the first few days here.

"Hey, Elle," he says. Two nights back we had stood impatiently and connected instantaneously.

"Hey," I beam back as the sun casts its scorching summer rays down hitting the concrete floor of the 'smoking cage' which now resembles a gorilla enclosure. The staff don't smoke with us. They would not dare to try mingling with us; we are sick, we are diseased. They smoke off the grounds at the entrance of the site, opposite a field of Shetland ponies. And us, well, we have the cage. Summer is in the air and I love the sweet scent that the greenery and fresh flowers emit, although I couldn't tell you the name of any of them. They are neatly planted and have a good range of summery colours, yellows and oranges and so on. My Mum is an expert when it comes to flowers. "How's it going?" I say.

"Not too bad. I went into town today and played Rebel Rebel on the juke box at Inns." Adam is looking dreamy. "It reminded me of you," he says.

"Ah, I love that song!" I shoot back, lighting my cigarette. We exchange personal accounts of craziness and I realise he is a man of many pleasures, a character who has really lived, wrecking everything that normal people admire, wrecking it just for fun by jumping at any opportunity for a good adrenaline kick… or just sending himself high and eccentric just because… just because this is how life should be lived, you know, like 'in the fast lane'. Kim used to swear by this saying.

Adam tells me allsorts that makes me smile and everything he says is truthful. Although crazy, he has much wisdom within himself. He tells me that when one lets go, like many do in here,

5

you realise how life should be anything but taken seriously. It is only when you let go of the ego that life can be enjoyed and happiness felt at its highest level. Sane people care too much to let go of their precious sanity. They treat it like it means something; I've started wanting to shake them until they become looser in their ways.

Adam is 'bipolar' if you like labels; personally I am losing faith in them. Spend a week in one of these places and you quickly learn that the staff have more issues than the patients. It's just that the patients are more raw, more defined and open, while the staff are uptight and slaves to society.

By the evening I have tired myself out; not mentally, for recently I have unlimited mental energy, but physically, yes. I say goodnight to the other patients (the ones I have spoken to) and take my sleeper ready to become mellow and slip away from the ward. Better yet, I feel one step ahead of the staff; they're currently enjoying keeping me a prisoner since the doctor instructed them that I am not allowed off the ward. I must see him again in five days and ask him to reconsider, which I assume he will reject just because he can. I have no faith in the human race and its ability to feel compassion. I have a sneaking suspicion that I am not of this Earth.

When I met with the doctor initially, I was a little too adamant that I was 'okay'; when someone insists overly that they are okay it's usually a lie. Also, I had a scar across my face that I had self-inflicted a few days before I was brought in. This was a strategic attempt to show the world that I wanted to become grotesque; but really the scar was just as superficial as I am.

Something else bad happened to me after my sister died. And let's just say it didn't work out, me living at my aunt's and uncle's house. But living there from three days after Kim's death up until coming into Fieldhead, as I stand now, I see that I learned a lot from them. I learned what it felt like to live with a family. To live in a stable environment, and with people who insisted everybody eats dinner together, who had lives that were all interconnected to one another's and not separate. Until it went wrong, and I do not know how or why. Maybe they never cared to begin with? Maybe it was my entire fault. Maybe I'll never know why they dumped me in the nut home. I thanked the Lord when I was dragged into here that I had grown up with my Mum, my poor Mum who couldn't afford a thing for me and my sister. I was so very thankful that things were not luxurious, that we ate corned beef sandwiches and wore hand-me-down dungarees that had more than had their wear from cousins, that things were not easy.

Never be envious of anyone, okay? No matter how it looks, often people who seem perfect are deeply damaged and masters at covering their insecurities and faults up with nice things.

I glimpse my reflection as I slip my night gown on. I have lost a lot of weight over the past few months. Prozac is a wonder drug. I look slightly unwell but I totally love this look of fragility. I wash my face and clamber into my ready-made bed. The beds have non-inflammable mattresses, which mean you stick to them during the night if the cover slips down. It often does if you toss and turn, which is very commonplace among patients on the ward. The way the sheeting is tucked in tightly reminds me of being in my bed at my mother's when I was younger; the bed covers were always too tight and often Laura Ashley-style designs that I disliked.

The room is bland and the ward decorator had an evident liking for pastel blues and white. The door has a window so staff can monitor your every move; this is a slight exaggeration but nonetheless I cannot help being angry when they shine a flashlight into my eyes every hour during the night. They do not take any care to be less direct with the flashlight and at times it stings my drowsy eyes, at which point I groggily tell them, "I'm not dead, so all is good."

The lights go out and the sleeping pill takes its timeless toll... The wall clock ticks a countdown for night's enticing illusions, lulling me into a false sense of security, convincing me that monsters cannot get me at night-time, just because I don't believe in them. As Luna's beams shine onto the laminated flooring, I feel glad, I am safe, yet I feel on edge. It's a good edge, a precipice, and if I fall over I'll never return. I'll never be sane again. The witching hour approaches. It is almost predatory. The ticking of the clock intensifies...

I fall far away, spiritually. Physically, my body jerks on the ward as my spirit self is transported to the urban city. The sky is a rich palette of violets and purples, slightly watery above the skyline. It's nice to see a horizon bleeding colours that are not red.

I float down the maze of cobbled streets, the street lamps looming over me, and I see Mel standing waiting for me with his hands in his pockets; he is the companion I created, a personification of my own melancholy. He is beautiful. And it is rare I deem any man at all beautiful. But Mel is so beautiful that it brings tears to my unusually emotional eyes.

He leads and I follow. Feeling ice cold, I feel deathly and sick, but I am well. Yes, I am so very well. I am one of the Fae people and tonight Mel looks happy to see me; he leads me past the city of dead streets, through to the towering woods on the outskirts. I fail to recognise this place at all. "Up there," he says, pointing to the top of the hill. I make the journey all alone, see an oak cabin and realise I must go there to announce an upcoming death. So I glide along softly, feeling the breeze caressing my cascading white locks, feeling the moonshine, up the hill with great ease. I consider, briefly, that the moon has lulled me into madness, and I pass that thought off as quite possibly true.

Upon reaching the cabin, I am captivated visually by a ghostly girl, young-looking, I presume early teens perhaps. As I glide over to her, I notice that blood is oozing from her matted light blonde hair.

"Are you okay?" I offer, as a means to figure out her state.

She unties a scarf from her neck and I see a deep gash. Seated on a wooden stool, she begins weeping but is mute in doing so. I comfort her and begin to empathise with her; she has bruises all over her body and I ask who did this to her and she points her long bony finger to the cabin, where I see a man through a window with the shutters wide open. I look at the girl's ivory face, so innocently ruined with red marks and bruises and her large blue eyes looking at me for comfort. I look away, back at the man inside. He has a stunningly wicked smile, a champagne flute in his hand, and although he is fairly attractive in a conventional way he has an ugly manner about him.

I glide towards the open shutters as the girl halts, silently sobbing. I put my hands before me where the glass that separates the open air would be, and screech in a malevolent fashion. I become ugly and haggard as I descend into harsh pools of tears and my pitch is high, so he turns to see me, at once dropping his champagne flute. He runs to fetch an axe but slips on the shattered glass, falls backwards, thudding harshly on the tiled floor with blood oozing from his head where he has cracked his skull. His numb skull, now he is null and void.

Relief floods through me as the screams have let out some pent up anger of mine, but as I turn to the girl she is weeping again and rocking back and forth in a self-soothing fashion. I notice another stool is now next to the stool she is perched on. I take a seat there, a golden harp to my left and a dreary scene of forestry to my right past the young girl, and although I am no harpist I take it up and play beautifully, angelically. But her tears do not cease and somehow I know they never will. I perch myself next to her, since a beautiful harp melody is not enough for her, stroke her head and wipe her tears. I beg and plead for the angels above to return my sister. I beg and my heart hurts and throbs.

A nurse shakes me. I awake abruptly

"Are you okay?" she asks, feigning kindness.

"What?" I ask, disorientated.

"I heard screaming noises. You should tell the doctor about your nightmares," she says.

I groggily respond, "No I shouldn't, he doesn't deal with un-earthly matters." I then pull the thin sheets over my head and she leaves. For some reason, I wish she would have stayed and comforted me. I actually dislike her and want to tell her to get lost most of the time, but sometimes we all need a mother figure after nightmarish hours. So I ask Mel to come and stay with me for the night. I don't want to be a banshee. I don't want to be tragic. I like the look of the banshee and I guess a banshee's nature is apt as my soul has now made a connection with death. But although tragedy is highly romanticised it is not for me... I pray. Mel is one who loves death. He loves suicide. He spends the night whispering sweet nothings in my ear, seductively sedating me, so I sleep well.

THE TREE OF DOOM

The fox said to the badger,
"Look up at the tree,
it's the tree of doom,
it's the only one we see."

The crimson grass was tainted.
The fox rolled his eyes,
"Are we to ask the wise old owl?
Come, for he awaits."

Three hundred and sixty degrees did Mr Owl's head spin,
a blank stare he gave.
Their answer there in one.
How was this done?

So the badger suggested,
"We could ask the tree
why it has such a peculiar
anatomy."

For the tree itself would surely know...

The tree was more than willing
to whisper through the wind,
caressing injured parties.
What an odd form of art.

"Sit, creatures, if you want me to begin,"
it announced with sincere blows.
"I do not hold leaves, my branches are too brittle."

It smiled…
"Besides, how could I hold leaves?
My branches are full of death."

It grew louder…
"You dumbfounded animals,
why such looks of remorse?
Everything comes back to nature,
I merely hold empty vessels."

"Are you the tree of doom?"
enquired the curious badger,
daring to make a sound,
feet rooted to the ground.

One branch then tumbled down,
the creatures' breath ended,
their skulls smashed,
bodies cracked like the tree's soul.

Hanging on its branches,
the decapitated animals' necks did sway,
never to see another day.

"Forgive me, Mother Nature!"
the tree cried out.
"I am the tree of doom."

(Scribbled down during Week One)

TWO

CHILD OF THE WILDERNESS

I am not what I appear. I am not the product of a defective home, nor did I grow up on the streets of some council estate built to keep its residents in the same houses for the rest of their days confined to comfortable misery. Some residents never leave their estates, dull from the moment they enter the world until the moment they leave. Well, not me. The dismal streets of Eastmoor would become a kind of puzzle, for how does one escape this life on these stolid streets with rows of houses filled with families with the best intentions but absent of any ambition beyond the town centre? I often strained to come up with any strategy that could deliver my soul from this confined future laid before me. Then I had a eureka moment around the age of eight; I came up with the most rational strategy that I could, being so young and clueless. I would sculpt a parallel universe to my liking.

It went like this. I would ascend into illusory clouds and be transported to a wilderness where I was a survivor of an inattentive family: a stepdad who was a damaging character and my playful sister who would be better off without me around, little me and my prim and proper mannerisms, my selective muteness and my demands to be noticed more. I loved my family, so this is why I stayed and left at the same time.

The parallel world would save me from being corrupted and keep my soul pristine. So I added many elements to the other world where I would live; I added mountains with winding, glistening streams whose waters ran with liquefied love. Its skies were iridescent spheres, scattered with stars that watched over the woodland's inhabitants. The night sky was the most magnificent masterpiece of all, if you ask me. During the daytime the amorphous cotton wool balls in the sky became a focus of my attention as I would lie back with a pack of wolves and try to figure out whether I knew I was in a parallel universe. If you have ever felt misplaced – well, maybe it's because you are? Maybe you have just slipped into a parallel universe that is an only slightly off-centre of your usual world.

When I went to school I would sit and tap my foot, looking out of the window and continuing my drawings of wolves. These wolves I knew from Clementine Woods. These wolves I knew personally. Clementine Woods is filled with pastel pink blossomed trees that sway gently to the ground; they land with precision, because although you may not know it, nature is very precise. Trees are sweet-tempered and mild-mannered. You can talk to trees through the wind, but you have to listen openly for there are a thousand different ways that nature can reply to you and you will usually only be tuned in to one or two ways.

Pink blossomed trees remind me of weddings. Kim used to marry the boy across the road when we were children; she would stand and smile as the boy next to her looked a little bored, while his sister and me would throw blossoms over them in childish exultation. Kim's cheeks would turn exceptionally red and I would wonder why she was blushing, as this would be about the eighth time we had staged this wedding. Her husband would then run off with his dog and his sister, and me and Kim would continue our day as normal, living in an invented fable made just for us.

I got stuck for a long while... In fact, I still am; I am betwixt a fictional world, the fable world of ghosts and ghouls and animated wolves, and the world where I am expected to become a nobody like everyone else. I always longed to make my name more than a word. I wanted my name to become associated with a certain sentence, such as: 'Elisa? Yes, she is an excellent mathematician', or 'Elisa? She is so beautiful', but not 'Elisa... who's she?'

Kim always wanted to be a shopkeeper as we grew up. I wanted to be someone whom people noticed, not a shadow. When I went off into Clementine Woods I would come back with a big grin on my usually glum face. I would then become more talkative but only at home, when nobody could hear me speak.

When I was around eight years old I was really speaking only to my Mum and my sister. Though if you count screaming as speaking, then I would speak at my Mum's boyfriend, Neville, because he was a bully. He favoured Kim. I did not begrudge her this in any way, but I did however hate him with a passion. His favouritism was probably due to the fact I was highly sensitive so did not engage with him as he tried to 'entertain' us; I hated being grabbed, or touched in any way, so when he tried to spin me around I would scream blue murder and become very upset. My Mum understood my sensitivities and voiced them to him, but he never took it on board. I would tell Kim my thoughts about him and she would nod and agree; we both disliked him. He didn't treat my grandma very well either, and she died shortly after we moved to Horbury (so Neville could be closer to his family who lived there).

At the end of our back yard was a fence, which had wooden planks lined up to separate our house from a huge, posh garden and an immaculate house that belonged to two rich, attractive old people whom Kim and I used to sell raffle tickets to. They had a golden retriever and it used to poke its head out of one of the loose planks. Me and Kim used to pet it, smiling, she with her cute, goofy smile and me with my chubby cheeks, round and rouge. I hated them. The golden retriever was friendly and would come when we whistled for it, much to our amusement, with its tongue hanging dumbly. We would hear it barking before it came and my Mum would shout for me to come away from the fence as I was allergic to dogs, but I would look at her stubbornly and refuse, because I disliked her orders. Faye, who was our baby sister, would be fast asleep in my Mum's arms as Kim and me ran around barking like children who should be in a nut house, loud and wild and unchained. Now Faye was born, we had more time to get away with being naughty.

The start of the new school was an experience that hit me harder than most; Kim made friends quickly and easily while I struggled somewhat. In my own universe, I grew dismal and hopeless. I began trying to play with Kim and her friends after school, but during school I was teased and mocked and felt that my torment would be eternal. Then I did make friends with one girl; her name was Samantha Sykes and I thought she was the most beautiful girl in the class. I was speechless and severely bewildered when she first spoke to me. Her mother then brought her round to our house which was a few streets away.

I was lucky after a fashion, because meeting Sammy and hanging out with her was worth putting up with the six hours I remained silently at a desk, looking out at the grim playground and dreaming of Clementine Woods and dining with wolves. I liked her because she was fun and she drew me into a world that ran in the opposite direction from my own. I was rigid in my imagination and she was liberal, with unlimited energy and originality it seemed. When I started hanging around with her, I kept my alternative world at bay and allowed myself this gift of friendship. It was a first for me and I was self-conscious with this friendship, but then it blossomed into something marvellous and charming. I was no longer Elisa the loner, I was Elisa with the best friend who was fun and intelligent and popular. And as we ran through horse fields, we vowed to set the gypsy horses free to run with a soaring eagle if they pleased, and I felt genuinely happy in another's presence, for real. I had only experienced happiness when I was alone up until this point, because I could not figure out others' intentions too well so disliked being around them.

Sammy, Kim and me would play together. Sometimes we played with magic and paganism, which Sammy introduced to me; the concept of magic had always been pretty foreign to me, so this was very exhilarating and fresh. We went on delving into magic as year by year we grew without realising it; we were soon teenagers, looking at each other in Sammy's bedroom with blades at our wrists, eyeliner down our faces, and the idea of love being so utterly heart-wrenching and painful that we just could not go on. We pressed the blades against our skin, confessing that we were relieving our heavy emotions, our love to our first teenage boyfriends. It was also in fashion among the alternative kids to have arms marked with neat, superficial gashes.

Sammy showed me how to be a person and how to cope with high school. Throughout junior school she had defended me when others cursed me intensely with insults that inflicted immense pain into my already wired-wrong head. She taught me how to be authentic and generally not give a damn about people's opinions; although I did give a damn, in fact I cared so very greatly that I was called a freak and shunned not just by the popular kids in school but even the lower ranking kids. I learned to feign not caring and, without realising, it would turn into me really not caring, not being hung up on being called a weirdo, but eventually after years turning into apathy. Sammy showed me how to be a good kind of weirdo - not the bad kind, like the freak who is secretly envied for their guts and opinions - and how to do it well, in black lace, heavy boots and gothic clothing. She taught me how to really blend in with the misfits and the alternatives. I was a pretender like they were but I was happy with this new stance, and we revelled in the insults that were thrown at us; to us they were roses and we were giving a good performance, our words deathly and our costumes morbid.

From the golden girl with cherry lip-gloss, I unfortunately turned into someone my mother disliked and Kim copied (Kim and I were becoming very close at this point). I turned into a freak with a dog collar and my new phrase to shoot back when I was called 'geek' or 'weirdo' was "Drop dead", which seemed out of character with my usual passive and silent self. But this was only when I was with Sammy or my other friend, Sophie. When I was alone, I was the defenceless, weird wallflower that withered inside emotionally.

Clementine now became a thing of the past. I was a child of the wilderness and I should have been brought up by howling canines in Clementine's woods. I never quite lost my spirit guide completely, this guide being whichever wolf I was reading about at the time. But I grew further away from nature. I tossed aside my old ideas as too flowery, too far removed from my teenage self who yearned for experimentation with drugs, alcohol and the odd opposite sex.

So I threw away my true self. I threw away my identity, my identity as a 'child of the wilderness', one whose traits were wolf-like and always loyal to oneself. My identity as a teenager was fickle and changed, as one does in the teens, every week. As I grew, I did nothing to figure out who I was because I was too influenced by my surroundings, moulding me into something I do not know the name of. I just know that I am something disfigured, disabled, a portrait that could have been magnificent gone wrong by adding too much to the painting so that little by little it became something ugly. This is me inside.

I sit now in my sombre mood, my past ancient and lost, and I feel my spirit is a good few centuries old yet I have learned nothing. The hospital door looks final with its little shutter window, alarming and displeasing; it is safe in here but I feel scared. I feel forsaken. And although I look into my past, my present and my future all at once, I am still none the wiser and have not an inkling of courage within myself to explore any more. At least, not tonight...

So I relinquish my responsibility to do so by permitting the heavy light of the moon to carry me into Clementine, where I spend the night in a body I recognise as my chubby child-like self. The wolves welcome me with a howl that echoes throughout the mountains and carries vibrations of mystical hope, and I laugh because Kim and Sammy are here tonight and they are swirling around and they are not bleeding. I thank God they are not bleeding.

The wooded area where I find myself is thick with greenery that is lit by fireflies that waltz and flicker, disorientating me somewhat in a dazzling kind of way. Pink tree houses are built into these tall trees that reach the clouds, a pristine kind of state that one just dwells in.

I stroke the wolves as Kim and Sammy laugh in the background. I recall that they have distinct personal laughing styles, and I remember each style well. Then I awake and there is no laughter, there is no Kim nor Sammy, and the pristine state of being... well, that was just these hospital walls seen through delirious sleep lenses. In a way, I thank God I am not the chubby, tormented child I used to be. But I would also die to relive any of those tormented days, because Kim and Sammy were there then. I was almost there then.

Amongst the sea of daunting trees
during winter's cloudy sleep,
I am beckoned beyond the grave,
to hear the wild ones weep.

They speak of nonsensical things.
And by the stream, flowing pure amethyst,
drenched in nature's purest springs,
I hear harmonious strings
and these things,
the wings of creatures unknown.
Their dance has a violent undertone,
the groan of the unknown.

by Lacey Jayne

THREE

A VAMPIRE ON THE WARD

You can sit
and you can pray,
but godless hearts
will wither away.

Well, I tried praying and it didn't work. I think the supposedly benign God has given up on me. For the past three days I have had many adventures, involving me being attired as a hag in rags and shrieking in people's faces... If you are wondering whether my mind has completely derailed, well, my answer to that would be "Absolutely!" However, this is not to the point where I believe I am a banshee in this world but, yes, in another one.

My other world is a city with nothing beyond it. I presume it will always be this way, never evolving beyond its borders because there is nothing beyond them for anything to evolve into. This is a shame for the residents and wildlife, and also for me if I ever get stuck in a dream and cannot return or wake up. My spirit visits this city approximately an hour after the Zopiclone has been administered. I swallow it compliantly from a tiny, thin paper cup, with both wariness and curiosity in equal measure - curious

21

because it brings me into an occult dream world quickly and easily, and I am fascinated by what I could become.

I go for a cigarette and engage in small talk, staring into the night sky for a short while. The stars are disorderly, chaotic and spread across the sky as though someone has thrown a bucket of stardust over a dark indigo backdrop. I breathe in the summer-scented greenery from beyond the cage bars. The moon's light is dusky and pale, pink clouds covering it as though the moon is not ready to come and light up the shadows just yet. Across my curious face is a particular question: why must the sky darken and does the moonlight cast down anything other than insanity, particularly when it is full? I look into the sky at the disorderly stars and I know I am gazing into the past.

Then I go and change into my bedclothes and as I mellow out I fall through the violet sky of delight and reach land safely. A concrete landscape. I am weightless. I then go to find Mel. He is so magnetic, a silhouette in the city lights. As I grow closer he turns to me with his divine eyes, his thick eyelashes and soft lips; we French kiss and then he leads me through a nicer bit of the city where I see balconies and brandy, upside-down smiles and buskers playing jazz and wearing outlandish clothes they bought from a charity shop. People look once, then twice, and pass me off as 'something paranormal'; we make our way through the upper class area gradually reaching the lower class with its graffiti streets and right-way-round smiles.

Last night in particular was a very strange event indeed. In fact when I awoke I sat bolt upright in bed and pulled my journal out from under my pillow, which was damp with sweat, to document all I encountered in this visit. And this is what I wrote…

> I am a banshee tonight and I have just returned to the ward where all is dead. Golden silence (well, more brassy) surrounds me, weaving through the dark corridors

like a deadly gas ready to intoxicate sleepers or restless insomniacs, ready to put intrinsic questions into our tiresome minds. The silence rouses within me a deep existential curiosity, one that cannot be satisfied, I find, when I am in this vessel.

I have warned a woman of her death. I felt satisfied that she would be expiring very shortly and I don't know why I felt satisfied but I did… She had children, she had a life. I was in a state of foreboding as I entered her perfect little home and her little picket fence clung on to my flowing dress, begging me not to alarm her or take her from her perfect life of rose bushes and cupcakes. I pulled my dress off the wood and glided through the sprinklers into the open front door, to see this woman in her mid-thirties sitting and drinking a mug of Horlicks and watching some romcom film in her living room. The room was a floral haven and this, combined with clichéd laughter from the television that vibrated into my heart, made me feel slightly nauseous.

I at once began my banshee wail. She jumped almost out of her skin, then screamed at me, telling me I must leave at once. I did, but I only left because Mel came inside impatiently and tugged at me telling me that he was growing cold waiting outside…

Me and Mel went for a walk around the weird city then and noticed that every street seemed equally as dead of any passions as the streets that I grew up on. Yet the streets I grew up on were always perceived as hopeful through my eyes as a little one. This city is mainly only lit by the moon and stars, rather than artificial light. This is pleasing because one can see only what one needs to see in the moonlight.

Me and Mel dined in silence at a late night café where we were served cherry pie and wine. It was a chocolate café and I was tempted to order Baileys but Mel told me he needs to watch his figure, at which I frowned as his figure is very trim. I told him he looked handsome, he told me I look pretty, and then I awoke into my hospital bedroom at 3 a.m. which is a significant time; but don't be presumptuous and look for some significant meaning in a significant time because sometimes there is no meaning that can be applied to yourself.

I don't know why I awoke but since I am now awake I thought I might as well write.

Reading back what I wrote now, I feel a little unsure in myself - am I doing the right thing by warning people of upcoming deaths, their own deaths? Am I a bad person in a world where I can get away with my badness, or am I simply a harbinger who needs to be around? I wonder if being warned of your own death would be useful? I wonder if my sister would have appreciated a warning, if her death had had been the result of, say, a less aggressive attack. She cannot speak for herself and I don't want to attempt an answer of something entirely unknowable.

I walk out into the ward with my journal in my skeletal hand but I don't spend much time socialising today and my dancing, careless self has gone out of the window. I am not in a fluffy, carefree mood at all today, just a reflective mood. So I sit among the others in the main lounge and avoid eye contact with everyone just so I don't have to interact. Thankfully the daffodil girl is no longer on this ward, this one being Priory 2, but on Trinity which is a higher security ward and has been deemed more fitting to cope with her hacking away at her arms, almost right down to the bone.

Looking around, I notice that most patients just look expressionlessly into space. Some of them see things in this space, others do not. You can usually tell which ones do by the obscure grins on their faces. The less mentally impaired patients read 'real life' magazines and eat custard creams, sloppily dunking them into their midday teas and coffees. I despise real life mags. One tall, lanky patient with greasy black hair stands in the middle of the room, looking up at the TV screen on the wall in astonishment.

"Look, it's a talking candle," he says through his toothless grin. As he turns around I look down into my journal hoping to be tugged through a vortex into its pages.

He is animated and oblivious to others' thoughts about his peculiarities. But the patients are happily watching Disney's Beauty And The Beast. It is one of my favourite films, and in fact Kim and I watched it many times when younger. I used to sing along boldly to the songs throughout and Kim used to look at me with one eyebrow raised and her head slightly tilted to the right. I have always longed to live my life out in a musical; I have always been a theatrical character, while Kim was more down to earth. If I had to to choose one musical I could live in forever, it would be Phantom Of The Opera, Andrew Lloyd Webber's version, and I would play the role of the Phantom not because I want to be a man but because men tend to have more charm and wit about them than women. I wish there were no such thing as opposite genders and we were genderless, kind of like aliens I guess, in a world where we are like plants and can reproduce by ourselves.

I read a few pages of my journal and come across one of Kim's many poems, Soar With The Angels. The poem troubles me a little, making me wonder if it is possible that one's spirit can foresee one's own physical time of death; the conscious mind may not be aware of this but just the spirit alone? But if one's spirit were connected with the mind then maybe one would know that death would be having its wicked way shortly, and know so in a conscious way.

I scribble my thoughts down frantically and I can tell that the scratching of pencil on paper is irritating the staff, so I continue.

> Who believes that a girl can turn into a doll? Dolls may become possessed by evil spirits or lost spirits but not an actual physical transformation like I witnessed. This is rare because it is inhuman. It is more common though than most may realise; you know the rate of homicide.

I drop my doll theories and toy with the idea of my own doll-like appearance, as one of the patients here calls me 'Barbie' while asking if I would like a coffee from the trolley. Hmm, maybe an alternative Barbie, or maybe the Barbie who has been through the hands of a corrupt child and now has split ends and bruises.

Turning the thick pages of my journal, I reach Kim's poem. The poem makes my insides twist and churn in an undeniable sadness. My hands tremble and I don't know if this is from low blood sugar or actual emotion, because I do not understand how I can identify emotion. It is a mixture of physical reactions that often confuse me, mainly because they overthrow me and inside I stagger; the fine emotional skin I have tears and I am exposed, on my knees, vulnerable to infections and disease.

I tingle with discomfort every time I read anything Kim has written; it's like a voice from beyond the bluebell grave, and I hate it not because I dislike hearing Kim's words but because I dislike what she had written. What she has written is not bad. I find her writing touching and full of raw emotion, but I dislike it because she had much underlying suicidal ideation. I can't say that suicide is something I have ever disagreed with, but I dislike reminding myself of her secret love for suicide, due to the fact that I could never prevent much of the pain that caused her suicidal ideation. I myself have also always had a love for suicide and all that comes with the idea of it. We had agreed, however, that if one of us committed suicide then the other would follow immediately - I remember us saying this not just once, we often talked about it.

Much of Kim's pain was due to her circumstances. From the age of thirteen she was placed in care, then because Social Services are not very good at this they moved her around often after she 'failed to behave' in each of the places. I was in care too when I was fourteen for a year, and this is where I met Otak. The staff used to tell me off for 'bullying' him! No, I did not hook up with him at this point as he made me want to physically vomit. I hooked up with him several years later.

I was kicked out of my Mum's address at sixteen and lived with my first abusive partner; then when I broke free from his chains I went back to live with my Mum until I was again kicked out at around eighteen years old. This led to me taking my first overdose. After the overdose I went to live in a grotty hostel where I shivered half to death in the night-time with my mind being poked and prodded by some unseen force... it was depression and I bled internally.

Otak took me then and mended me - or so I thought. You see, I had no choice; he convinced me that he was a saint. He took me for posh cocktails that were secretly laced with lies and told me I should not cry. I told him I had been exiled by the world and he told me that if I were to go and live with him I would have a shot at becoming happy again. So that was what I did - because people want to be happy. Even though when they receive happiness it makes them either bored or sad.

Does my Dad feel any relief from such a poem, the one in the Prologue, a poem that speaks almost directly to him? I guess yes and no... I read Kim's cute covered diary after the funeral; we have both been avid writers and observers throughout our adolescence. I found Kim's diary, much to my disappointment, was empty of any events or even any references to me. I guess I wasted much time that I could have spent with her, taking pleasure in the way we finished each other's sentences. I wasted it on attempts to correct my own life by throwing myself in the deep and handing myself over to a barbarian.

Kim's poem seems to haunt me for the rest of my evening. Her words do not want to go unrecognised and this is why I write, for I cannot let her down, however dead she might be. When she is written about, it is as if the idea of her is being kept on life support. This could be viewed as a cruel thing to do, for the 'idea' of someone is often lacking in their key features, and images of the past are distorted. So I take a shower, a bitterly cold shower, to wash the eeriness of Kim's lingering words from my mind and it works. The shower room is bland and reminds me of a gym, because the button has to be pressed every minute or so which inevitably leaves you shivering for a few seconds before the water plunges out once more. I notice all the tiles lined up and I cringe at the fact this shower is shared by twenty-odd people. I run the soap over my dry skin and I wonder how it would feel to slip and break my neck on the soapy floor; the water trickles down the drain as I wrap a towel around my goose-bumped body, trying to insulate my skinny self. But I leave the shower room cleansed.

I then see a vampire aimlessly standing in the corridor. I have noticed him over the past few days as he is a guy who, you could say, has a complete heroin chic vibe to him, not intentional but an effortless grunge appearance. Slightly unkempt, he is leaning casually against the corridor wall next to his bedroom door with his headphones in and Black Sabbath blaring out. I am trans-fixed and as I walk past him to reach my room, which is parallel to his room, he seems unaware of his surroundings altogether.

I had tried to smile at him this morning as I noticed during dinner time yesterday (which was jacket potatoes with various toppings) that his eye contact is potent and deep. He has one of those soul-piercing looks, you know, the one where once eye contact with the person is made the soul is transparent and to him mine is wavering and weak. It is exclusively seen by the one with the soul-piercing eyes and this gives me a nice little kick of adrenaline, a shot that courses through my veins and makes my legs buckle slightly. I am being undressed with his eyes and my towel falls down metaphorically and I am bare and breathless. I sit down against my closed door facing him and the towel is wrapped around my violated skin and bones. He sits down too. And without breaking eye contact for a few seconds I recognise darkness within him. But it's not the dangerous kind.

His jasper eyes tell of a damaged soul. He has amorous eyes, 'amorous Tobias' I think, as I try my best not to get locked in this moment. I shake inside as his perfect brown, oval eyes and symmetrical face leave me locked in position, not daring to move a single muscle. I move my eyes around his face taking in this golden boy, his lips sculpted perfectly and slightly parted, his dark eyebrows simply sitting above his stargazer eyes. I smell him, he smells of sweat combined with hospital bedding that has not been changed for a good week and his smell is inviting. His eyes are deep and unfathomable; they are eyes that are lost in psychosis, this I know. Yet somehow I beg through my own eyes for him to see me through his own eyes, not through the tainted lenses of psychosis.

The bare corridor has only me and him occupying the space. The moment is surreal and is broken when a gay male member of staff pops his head around the corridor and shrieks,

"Medication time!" Tobias jumps up at once and I dart into my bedroom and slip my nightclothes on. We take our medication and I start to feel a slight sexual attraction to him. I kick myself for feeling this way, because I have an ingrained stupid belief that I still belong to Otak - and in a sense I do, because he has me locked forever in a cell of a mind that he created by causing me eternal grief.

The Zopiclone tonight induces a certain kind of sensual dreaming, in which I embark on a seductive dance of two hearts pounding against one another's chest, as legs entwine and gratification is felt by both parties - me and Tobias. We are both trying to devour each other's existence with kisses that are vampiric in nature, draining in a fashion but a draining where one wishes to be drained, and sacrificing one's own soul to be taken by the other, drinking up each other's energy until we are exasperated and dying, dying to become at one with one's lover. This is a very unhealthy way of thinking, but there you go. Some people are damaged and I am one of them. I hope Tobias is too.

I awake in cold sweats and a metallic taste in my mouth. I walk over to the mirror in my little PJ shorts and Hello Kitty tee. I pull my stripy socks up just over my knees then I touch my lips and see little droplets of blood form on my bottom lip... I feel electrified and see through the dim lighting into my mirror reflection where it has been subtly pierced. I look at my fingers and although it is dark I can see I have red liquid on them, only a modest amount, so I clamber back into my bed and pull the sheets over my head hoping to suffocate underneath them. I awake later and look in the mirror, accidentally knocking my cosmetics off the side. I feel spirited and smile to myself, but I cannot see the bite mark that was there last night.

Dear Kim,

I had a nightmare last night, like I have done pretty much every night since you were taken, and in a strange way I take comfort in the nightmares because sometimes you and I share a sentence or two before horror kicks in. I just want to say I am thankful for those precious conversations, because you don't visit me out of my nightmares.

I talk to you in my mind. I do so all the time and I never hear you reply. Maybe one day he will no longer gain access to my sleeping mind and the nightmares will turn into little talks that we can have? Kim, how did I get to be in Fieldhead? We often joked that I needed a room there but I am actually here. And I feel myself descending into a hypnotic kind of madness that I cannot quite place. Help me please.

Here is a scene I want to tell you about - it is real, this one. It's one of the factors that led to me coming in here. It was not straight after this that I was hospitalised but this was deemed to be one of my 'odd behaviours' that Auntie Anne and Uncle Arthur noted; they told the police after we got back from holiday about my 'manic behaviours'. Okay, here goes...

I walk between thick blades of emerald grass that almost reach my knees, at the side of the motorway, with glazed-over eyes and a hopeful mind, and this is because I am going to do a deal with Lucifer. I am on my way to your grave. It is 6 a.m. and the dawn is pulling through in a desperate attempt to begin today. But I cannot begin my day, I was awake all last night and I ate a little too much this morning.

Do you believe in Lucifer? I do, I've seen him. I have spent the last few weeks attempting to conjure him.

31

He can bring back the dead, you know. He can bring you back. Fancy that, you can reach your hand out of the soil and it would be, like, "Thanks people, you buried me alive." That would shock people, to say the least. Not me, because I know that this is not the end. As I tread through the weeds I see a police car shoot by in the corner of my eye. I continue with my wax-sealed paper deal. I wrote to Lucifer in blood this morning and now I am to bury the pact above your grave and see what happens. Even if you don't rise from the dead and step out of your coffin, I made it known on the pact, the piece of paper I am carrying, that you can always come to see me in spirit form. I am sick of you bloody in my dreams. I see your contorted face all the time. Sometimes I am back in the house of horrors, sometimes I fall onto your dead doll body and I cannot move.

The police car pulls up at the side where I am ploughing through the dewy grass, both focused and unfocused, fearful and absent. The police are vibrant-looking, the woman a little plump and the man a little lanky, and they insist on me telling them my name. I am not visibly crazy, I hope, but my demeanour tells a different story; so they bring me back to Anne's and Arthur's who then have a talk with me. They tell me I am unwell and I burst out laughing. I have never felt so well.

See, when you died I was very sad and I was sad for Sammy too but I survived and I think something chemically changed in my brain, for now I am awake and I spend every minute of my day appreciating the world around me and my new-found freedom. This is selfish and wrong. I should be depressed, Kim, and I am, but paradoxically I am also so very alive.

It was hard living with Otak. I could not breathe without receiving cruelties. I tell Anne and Arthur to calm their passions, and they tell me that unless I start eating an appropriate amount of food I cannot join them on holiday to Italy. Me and you used to starve ourselves together, do you remember? You didn't need to and I should have stopped you because you were already thin and pretty. I promised Anne and Arthur no more pacts to the devil or starvation diets. I promised but it meant nothing - I have never been one to keep promises besides the ones I made to you.

I look back on our little talks and I analyse your every micro-expression.

I wonder, did you make it to Heaven?

BPD (OR, AM I REALLY ME?)

Okay, so to me Borderline Personality Disorder was at first an explanation, then at times a pathetic excuse for my fucked up persona. BPD is Heaven and Hell, it is light and dark, it is also abstract and confusing and if you ever meet a borderline individual you will probably perceive this deep confusion – a confusion about who we are. I do not know the basic identity of myself. I do not know my likes or my dislikes; they change all the time, quicker than the weather changes on a moody day, in fact sometimes on a minute to minute basis.

Everything is black and white, so many things in life that happen to be grey are not processed. This makes things hard but I am learning much from Mel: Mel is a grey character and this is because long-lasting sadness is not black, it is not despair, and it is obviously not white because that would be happy, it is just grey and like a thick fog of noisy confusion.

33

Anyway, here is a simplified list of the symptoms taken from the Internet after much research, for the purposes of showing you my condition. It's said that there are four groups of symptoms:

1   Impaired emotional control: excessive and poorly regulated emotional responses, especially anger, that change rapidly.

2   Harmful impulsivity: impulsive behaviours that are harmful to the self or to others, such as spending, excessive use of alcohol or drugs, self-injurious acts (e.g. cutting), physical aggression and sexual indiscretion.

3   Impaired perceptions and reasoning: suspiciousness, misperceptions, an unstable self-image, a poor sense of one's identity, and difficulty in reasoning under stress.

4   Disrupted relationships: tumultuous relationships with a person close to one that vary from extreme fear of abandonment to episodes of excessive anger and the desire to get away from that person.

If you ever meet me you will fall in love with my character, this goes without saying. You will fall in love with the way I come into your life and provide you with an intensity that you will typically mistake for intimacy, and you will feel immense love for the way I start to worship the gravelly ground you tread upon. I will inspire you and make you feel alive.

You will love me but the dark, sad truth, however, is that I do not share this love with you; I am intense because my emotions are intense but it won't be long before I back away and leave you wondering what you did wrong. I will become aloof and distant because I do not take pleasure in intimacy - it makes me want to hurt myself. You will wonder where the child-like girl who provided you with much excitement initially has gone... the laid-back, easy-going individual who was all rainbows and pots of gold...

You think that if you remain by my side this same person you fell in love with will come back. You think you can fix me? You cannot, and that amazing person you met... well, she was a facade to draw you in. Did I ever love you? I wish I could say I did but I don't know what love is. My advice to you is, don't try to fix what is permanently broken.

So if you meet me and you see my personality as something you want in your life, something thrilling - don't be fooled for I will always be a borderline bitch. And to be borderline means unable to experience love in an adult sense. I do not feel love the way you do. You won't save me. I can't save myself either.

I have a blessing and a curse bestowed upon me. It is called BPD.

FOUR

THE BOGEYMAN AND BLACK-EYED CHILDREN

The Bogeyman is under each patient's bed at night. Or in their wardrobes. I know this is so based on my own experiences, and the Bogeyman - if you do recognise him, which is difficult because he is usually somewhat like a giant black blob merged into night shadows - will turn into your worst fear... When I encountered him he turned into a pounding, bloody, ravaged heart organ on the floor. I didn't know what to do when I saw this so I screeched out. The heart was still beating but it was clearly running out of oxygen or life essence, which is love.

This is clearly symbolic of fear of 'a broken heart'. It appeared gruesome and looked like something you would find at a butcher's shop; it had been hacked into and was a very messy organ just to be lying around on my floor. It would be a safety hazard for one thing - if a nurse walked in unknowingly she could slip and severely hurt herself. She probably might not mind, though, as she could then claim sympathy. (I myself am a claimant of sympathy to the deepest degree humanly possible; I am doing so for what happened to my sister and friend. After all, does this not leave me with a huge disadvantage? Having no heart other than a melancholic, traumatised one is very disabling.) The moonshine was highlighting every inch of the mangled-up heart so I shouted at Mr Oogey Bogey for leaving me with such a thing, or becoming such a thing, depending on how his anatomy works.

"Curse you, you horrible blob!" I said, as I picked up the heart and placed it in my bin. My hands were stained and liquefied with the blood, or life force. The thumping it was making eventually caved in and it became still and deceased.

I had to eventually call upon a member of staff (this being 2 a.m.) and ask for a mop. She walked me back to my room after I told her the urgency and the facts, that the patients should be alerted to Mr Oogey Bogey. "He's a very bad blob," I said. The night nurse told me to "Come back down to Earth and stop being so childish." I guess Mr Oogey Bogey must have cleaned up the mess because when we approached my room the laminated flooring was squeaky clean and nothing was in the bin besides empty biscuit wrappers and vomit. Am I schizophrenic, you may be wondering by now? Did trauma turn me psychotic? No, I just became exaggeratedly imaginative.

This was my first experience with the Bogeyman and the second was much more intense. I saw the silhouette of a girl playing the trumpet outside and I knew right away that this was my sister. See, me and Kim ended up joining a brass band when we were around the age of ten (there is a year and a half age gap between us and she's younger); we weren't impressed as I wanted to play the flute and her the keyboard, but Mum thought it was a good idea - up until we borrowed two trumpets from the band and made as much racket as possible in our bedrooms. At that point my Mum suggested we join the recorder group at school.

I wish for Kim's sake that I had been a child prodigy, a musical genius, for then I would play her the harp until she rose from her grave, enchanted by my mellifluous notes and she would perhaps come to rescue me from the Looney Bin. And also from Mr Oogey Bogey's tricks. She often did so when we were younger; she would calm me when I became terrified of the bedroom lights going out.

Where was she now?

I climbed back into my bed when the nurse left and I fell silent to the fact that she was really not around. And I briefly fell out with her in my head for deserting me to join Heaven's crew of the passed-on ones. And if you have ever lost a loved one to death you will know this feeling; if not, imagine the feeling of abandonment you feel in childhood when your mother leaves you, or your father (my father left me and my sister when we were still toddlers). Well, this feeling of abandonment comes into the equation and you cannot forgive the person who died for dying even though this is completely irrational. I have always been quite rational in most ways but when one has lost a loved one to death, irrationality becomes a way of living. I let tears trickle down my face in my silent room where no-one knows I am alive and helplessness submerges deeper into my psyche.

I did not cry during the funeral. I did not cry because it had not happened to me and I was distracted by talk of the Lord and the Jesus songs that were sung by all of us sinners, and I thought for a second, 'How dare people sing holy songs with lips of poisonous guilt?' Guilt for never being there for Kim. And at this point I looked up away from the black lace and pretentious flower arrangements; I looked above me to the structure of the building and faintly hoped for the building to collapse on all the fabrications that were present on this day, this day of guilt and grief.

I did not cry. I did not cry because I am not a person who cries. Everybody else cried and this baffled me. Why cry when there were no reminders of Kim at the funeral to trigger tears, just a coffin with a doll inside, and people around who had not ever been a big part of Kim's life. I cry tonight though, and I lie in bed thinking and the thought hits me that one does not see their lives flash before their eyes before they die. I did not see anything when Otak stood before me licking a bloody knife, telling me I was next. Sometimes I want to cry like a baby, but with no-one to pull me back together I cannot afford to fall apart with watery eyes and a sniffling nose.

I remember when me and Kim were teens we often laughed and joked that we were pretty damn cold and we decided this was a good thing. "We are like Janine from EastEnders," Kim would say and I'd reply, "Yep we are but fuck it." We both had this attitude problem but it was okay because it was us against the world. In fact our attitude and closeness often got in the way of relationships I had with boys throughout my adolescence, because I would tell them very sternly, "My sister comes first." I was also over-protective of her in our mid-teens and when she ran away from her foster home I would tell her to go home because I wanted her to be safe and away from night stalkers or bottles of cheap wine.

I was unruly myself but this worked both ways; we were both unruly and wild yet we wouldn't let each other become what we were ourselves, even though we were both the same. And people often mistook us as twins. Just before we went into the care of Social Services (which was a decision completely out of my mother's hands) we were together every single day and we were kindred spirits, both complicated yet simple people who enjoyed imitating each other. We went through all our teenage phases together, we spoke at the same time and often we would jest how we were 'too alike for it to be true' but it was true. It was genuine and it was never going to change. We were never going to change. Not ever. Until we did. Until it did.

We were fiercely loyal to one another, which brings me to the disappointment - why can I not bring myself to get back to her? Tonight I sleep with these memories running through my head because when I sleep now it is either a very deep nightmarish sleep, or a light fleeting one that flits between memories. If I play the trumpet, maybe I will be transported back into childhood. So as my head becomes light and the ward evaporates, I wish for one even though me and Kim played terribly. I think I would wake the whole ward up... though I want to remain in my new friends' good books.

You know something though: Kim and I were the black-eyed children once. When I tell you things, try not to take them too literally because I often walk between worlds. I walk and dip in and out of a dream ocean. Tonight I gently lower myself into this dream, wetting my toes first, bobbing my foot in and out as I feel the tepid swishing around my toes that I wiggle. Looking down into my reflection in this ocean, I see through the clear crystalline waters a dream duplicate of me. But behind me is Mel and he pushes me into the ocean. The hospital vanishes and we plunge together into a sea of Zopiclone dreams.

First I will explain what it meant for us to be black-eyed children...

Me and Kim were once attired in old-fashioned promises of what life could offer us when we became officially 'grown ups'. These promises were outdated, involving love and marriage and such disillusioned things. We only went to strangers' doors when we felt separated from the world in our prepubescent years. I was very sickly. I wanted to be kidnapped and smothered with a pillow, while she wanted a new home. We loved our mother but we were lost spirits inside from a young age.

We went around together and our small bones felt so cold during those witching hours. We would slide out of our bunk beds and make it out into the night, with lost innocence lighting our way down streets of a broken neighbourhood. Our eyes became black and this was only to warn off night predators like paedophiles and the like. We could not switch our black eyes to normal coloured eyes when knocking on people's doors because we had to keep our wits about us and the person answering the door could also be a predator. We often got slams in our little faces. We appeared like twins, one spirit of two sisters, the spirit of two individuals attuned to one another more than the sky is attuned to the stars.

Tonight, stars are planted in the places they are supposed to be in and me and my sister must go and find a comforting place to rest our legs as we wander the streets, praying to stay children forever. We were clever children and we knew it must be done - we must stay as children if we were to survive in this world. We have just wandered from the woodlands that lead to a town of cheery faces and street lamps that give off a pink dusky light. The houses here are cottages because fairytale towns do not have houses filled with modern emptiness or large buildings of offices or anything like that; the town here is of non-existent people just living in their houses because they do not work and are mainly just housekeepers or gardeners growing food for their families. That way we also prevent the risk of GM crops' harmful effect on our bodies.

We approach a house that has a washing line strung up with various organs pegged onto it along with teddy bears, all of which look worn out and tatty. A little fish water feature is trickling and we are holding each other's small hands tightly as we look at each other and speak through telepathy. We ring the doorbell and who should answer but Mel and he invites us in; we smile at each other and step lightly over the welcome mat on the porch. I quickly link arms with Kim and feel glad that her body is warm. It's like old times when we linked arms as we walked to the shop with the money we had conned off old ladies by saying we were in need of charity. We then bought lots of sweets with this money, liquorice laces and violets.

Inside, the haunted-looking walls are filled with dolls that sit here there and everywhere. I dislike them, other than a few that remind me of people who have left me. Kim lights up when she sees a music box and when she opens it the ballerina spins around and Daisy Daisy plays followed by You Are My Sunshine, and I recall that my mother had a beautiful voice when she sang it to me and Kim in what feels like yesterday. Mel says, "Why are you dreaming of this, Elisa?" and I suddenly catch on that I am in a dream world right now...

"Mel, why have you turned up?" I say, as Kim continues to wander around the living room running her little fingers over the precious porcelain faces of the dolls that have cute rosy cheeks and little puckered lips.

"You have chosen to come here subconsciously," he replies, as he takes a teapot off the small marble table. "Tea?" he says, offering a china cup.

"No," I respond, and in my child body I feel a tantrum coming on, for I didn't want to be awakened from this sleep tonight.

"Don't get the lip out, Elisa. I just think you should return to your bed on the ward," he says, looking concerned.

"You know I can't think or talk about Kim when I am awake," I say, taking the china cup into my small hands, longing to grab Kim and run and run and perhaps never stop running.

"Yes, because you're too busy thinking of the other patients on the ward," he says.

"Not really. You know I haven't stopped writing and I write to her," I say. She doesn't seem to hear me.

"Look, just spend tomorrow writing about Kim - not just to her. Look at her, don't you think she deserves that?" he says. I look at her as she plays with the music box, singing its songs with her little whispery voice. She looks like a wisp that might disappear if I blink even once.

"Okay, I will do that. I only have half a heart, Mel - I need to find a lover to complete it or give you your heart back," I respond, feeling tearful.

"That can wait. You don't have to worry about when to give me that half back. Okay?" he says.

"Okay."

I feel the room become blurry and the ground I'm standing on is becoming tipsy and unsteady and I feel my heart tremble uncontrollably. I drop the tea cup, my body drops and I fall, this time into reality. Upright, I sit and cough and splutter from my smoker's throat, and see that Mel is slumped in the bedside chair, snoozing. I hate him sometimes.

melancholy
melancholic caresses
underneath ambivalent skies
when love no longer impresses
limerence, overwhelms then dies

and every star is languishing
beside Luna's fervent light
yes, melancholy is the dark, the night
mutual carefree devouring
we are absent of conventional plight

merging into raw emotion
the sullen stars begin to weep
wistful rapturous motion
the sky venturing through REM sleep

weary of gratification
but bodily fluids now combined
momentary satisfaction
rendering to what was pined

FIVE

WARD ROUNDS

I have to see the doctor today and this is a shame because I have a theory that he is not really a doctor but an imposter. I have spent all morning listening to schizophrenic ramblings. These would be enjoyable if I'd had an adequate night's sleep. My Dad once told me that his mother was schizophrenic. He said she used to claim she was married to a ghost, and when he was growing up she was in and out of the nut house.

Can this be true? Well, theoretically yes, one can be in love with a ghost, but technically not marry one because that might require a living arrangement under the House of God and for the ghost to be present physically. However one can definitely be married to a ghost in the sense of a lifetime commitment to the dead. She was in the old hospital called Stanley Royd, which was knocked down and rebuilt a few hundred yards up the road and called Fieldhead. Some of the old hospital's ghostly remains are in Fieldhead's on-site museum that's open on Wednesdays for patients to view the shackles and strait jackets, the padded cells and the records of patients' admissions for 'mental illness'. I use the term very loosely. The records are examples of how little people knew about mental illness and carry the label The West Riding Pauper Lunatic Asylum. So only paupers were crazy?

The doctor is sitting and looking at me as though he is concerned about me. I don't tell him of my nightmares. I don't tell him about any of my pain, I just sit and stare expressionlessly at him expecting him to read my mind because isn't that what doctors do?

There are two nurses present and these nurses are the old-fashioned kind, you know, the ones with outdated views on mental illness. They are well behaved when the doctor is present and probably convince everyone but themselves that their conduct is professional. Me and Adam noted that they really ought not to be working in a job they clearly resent. (Or maybe it is their wages that they resent?) They see the potential in many patients here; they see intelligence in us and creativity that they do not possess. Most crazies have star potential, because they can work with seemingly inexplicable magic. They work with the universe, not against it - the ones I have encountered so far anyway. It's a shame that these nurses are so unhappy, I think, as I look over at the round, frizzy-haired Ward Manager typing up the doctor's comments so far.

I don't feel a need to speak and I am jittery and can't sit still. Mel is not helping my nerves as he is pocketing various possessions from the doctor's drawer, various personal treasures that the doctor probably won't notice missing for some time. Mel is a kleptomaniac. He says he likes to steal because he is an adrenaline junkie.

"You look a little on edge?" the doctor says, shifting his enchanting blue eyes from the notebook he has on his lap to meet my uneasy eyes. He wonders why? He has just been babbling on about my sister's death for the past fifteen minutes and I'd be inclined to tell him to shut the fuck up if his eyes weren't quite so mesmerising.

"I am fine. I know what you're thinking. You think I am post traumatic, don't you?" I say honestly. He has a pale blue jumper on that matches his irises.

"I am not making any diagnoses, I just need to get a picture of your mental state in regards to the trial. Do you feel able to give evidence?" he asks.

"Of course I do," I say, shrugging my shoulders. I like to give off an invincible act; I also like to pretend I'm strong and although I'm told I am strong I know that I'm not. I know that people are basing this on my appearance and it's all an act. I am a brilliant actress. Truth is, most people who appear strong outwardly are inwardly dying.

"Okay, good. Have you `phoned your parents yet?" he asks, and his expression is soft but in a masculine way, so I feel bad for branding him an imposter. I thought he was an imposter because he is never seen around and Mel told me that he's probably an ex-patient who stole the real doctor's identity. This is a cruel thing to do, you know, to steal someone's identity; some of us are not lucky enough to have an identity. The doctor before me now appears nice. That is a doctor's job, though, to look all compassionate. And if he wasn't a professional, I would fall in love with his look.

"No, I haven't. My Mum wants to know where I am but she thinks I lied about what happened between me and my aunt and uncle - you have to remember that my uncle is her brother," I say.

"Okay, and what about your father?" he asks, narrowing his eyes.

"What about him?" The nurse looks at me and I despise all eyes being on me.

"Well, are you currently in contact with him?" he says, looking directly at me. My palms sweat a little.

"No, I am not," I reply, not really understanding what this has to do with anything.

"Last time we spoke you said that he had left you and your sister when you were a toddler, and that you had regained contact with him over the past few years. Do you get on with him?" he asks. I hate personal questions but I answer him fully.

"Me and my sister Kim managed to get in touch with my Dad and our half-brother who grew up with him a few years ago. I get on with him, yes, he's a funny guy." I slump back in my seat and begin tapping my foot. The carpet is rather dull.

"After your sister died..." he is speaking carefully, "did you start seeing him and your brother? I am just thinking that you are going to need a good support network over these next few months."

Support? I need no support. The only people who ever offered me support were my sister and Sammy. Mel looks offended by this statement and mutters something to himself. I ignore him but frown.

"Well, rest assured I will be okay. I'm going to `phone my Mum and Dad later," I say. He writes something down, then looks round at the large nurse who is typing as if to say, "Note this down"; then he returns his scrutinising attention to me once more. I am scowling at Mel now, trying to tell him through my eyes to leave. He picks up on this and jumps off the window ledge where he is perched and exits. He has a cigarette behind his ear so is probably going to smoke after he's emptied his pockets into my treasure box, an old shoe box where I keep all Kim's things such as sea shells, beaded jewellery and photographs she took of the gritty English coast that have times and dates printed on the bottom. They're a dispiriting kind of photos, edging on a hope-lessness that was clearly unintentional from Kim's eyes as she snapped the views through her social worker's car window.

"Well, is there anything you want to ask me?" the doctor says politely.

"No, not really. Except, I guess, how long am I in here for?" I say, although I am indifferent to the time scale.

"We will speak again next week. You have all your belongings from your aunt's and uncle's house, don't you? The police dropped them off. So now let's just concentrate on keeping you well for the trial and then finding you somewhere to live - how about going back to live at your mother's when all this is over?" he says.

I laugh a little and smirk. "Not an option," I say, and the nurses simulate a smile, the enchanting doctor smiles, jots a word or two down and nods as if to excuse me.

"Okay, well, you can go now if you like," he says kindly. Somehow I don't want to leave the room because I want to tell him he is beautiful. In case he doesn't already know. I want him to take me home and make me all better. I smile back and then get up to leave.

That evening I `phone my mother and it goes as predicted. She cries down the `phone and tells me that it's all my fault and that I am a liar. I have always been a liar. She tells me I am an abomination and always have been. I tell her to go fuck herself and then run into my room, I break down. I really break down.

Her words have bludgeoned me to death. Like they always did.

I sit and listen to Courtney Love's tribute song to Kurt called Dying. I play it over and over, needing the repetition to injure me, the breakdown of emotion during the chorus, and then the ending with Courtney's words, 'Remember, you promised me, I'm dying, I'm dying, pleeease... I want to, I need to beeee... under your skin.' I want the lyrics to become tedious and I want to snap out of this self-loathing. It hasn't worked after the song has played five times, so I cut and I cut and I bleed and I bleed all over my cute white summer dress and nobody comes to stop me. So I stop myself. I change and then go out for a cigarette.

I text my Dad, "Hey, how are you?" because I have to start the conversation with a standard question, in circumstances that are not so standard.

I engage in conversation with Liz, Carl and Adam and I look at them hoping they pick up on my inner need for comforting words; they don't and this is a good thing because instead they brighten me up. Tobias walks past and smiles, my whole world suddenly lightens and butterflies nauseate me. When I get back into my bedroom Mel is on my bed listening to Courtney Love, whom he hates (he says she killed Kurt). I tell him I'm a killer too. He asks how and I say, "I made mistakes that led to two girls being six foot under"; he tells me to shut the Hell up and it's not my fault.

I position my doll Harriet, whom I bought a few days ago, next to my pillow, straighten her scraggly hair and pat her Victorian dress down that has puffed out. The cleaners are not careful enough with Harriet. They should not even touch her and I screamed at them for this yesterday. As they left my room and I entered I told them, "Don't ever touch my fucking doll again!" I was then told that I am quite terrible and very immature, which I disagreed with but had to internally accept. I am 'like a toddler' in my angry outbursts, they say. I cannot help getting out of control when something irritates me; it's like I go back to the emotional age of a child and anger takes a hold on a volcanic scale so eruption is inevitable and very destructive. I was emotionally arrested - probably around the age of three.

In the art room, patients have just finished an occupational therapy session of arts and crafts. I pour paint all over the A2 paper, white and red mixed, and swirl it around with the brush making a warping kind of abstract design. It looks wrong, making a nice pink that I did not intend. I sit on the chair and I contemplate for an hour or so and I begin to feel mindful of my surroundings, of the smell of the paint, the brightness of the colours, the dull hue of the sky outside, the contrast of clouds to sky to city lines, the tower of the town's cathedral… I remember the way the clouds had parted as if torn by God's hands and a glow streaked the motorway roads that I found Otak driving me down not so long ago. I remember this and the need to jump out of the car to die.

So I unbuckle my seatbelt. Then Tobias knocks on the art room door. I hand him a cigarette and then I paint something I like.

I sit bolt upright in a hospital bed on the A and E ward. I am dead though. I am dead inside and cannot feel any blood flowing through my veins. In a sickly confusion, I recall being moved onto a day ward in Pinderfields General Infirmary, my mind crippled with a sickness I don't know the name of. I am vegetated, yet somehow I pick my heavy legs up, pull the side bars of the bed down, pull the drip out and climb off carefully. Somehow I slip my ballet shoes on too and head for the bathroom where I check myself out and the mirror confirms my fears. I am dead. I have bloodshot, hollow eyes and my arms and legs have gone blue.

They have been administering poison, depression liquefied, through the thin tubes. They must have done it thinking it was the proper treatment, thinking it was something to counteract the aspirins I took, but they have made a mistake. They have given me a mind sickness known to turn people into zombies. And now I am one.

Within a few minutes I decide that I must leave, so I try to but I bump into a security guard who escorts me back to my bed. I can't articulate anything so I let out a few groans of displeasure. I wonder if zombies can learn how to talk again; at the minute I am picturing living in my head forever 'til the fragile hands of time snap. I don't want this so inside I begin to kick and scream, but my body just won't have any of it and tears won't come out of my eyes no matter how hard I squeeze them tight. The nurses come and, as attentive as they are, they mistake me for a zombie too; they send the medical doctor through and again my mute state leads him to believe I am a zombie.

I see them discussing me in the office and wonder where they send people like me. I am scared. I am very scared. My heart can't be felt and I put my index finger on my wrist but there's no pulse. Have I killed myself? Or is it mind sickness? I know mind sickness is a state of walking through life in the 'inbetween'. We are zombies, we in the inbetween, though people don't fear us; they don't assume we will eat their brains, they don't see us as ravenous dummies, they just see us as people drained of life or don't see us at all... And we drift through life, the living dead. The real living dead.

The drip is reconnected and more depression is flowing into my veins. The woman across from me is the same, on a drip too, and I assume she is being administered with the same mind sickness. Although she has started pissing herself and the nurse keeps changing her. I hope I don't piss myself. I was uncon-scious and dreaming when they attached me to my drip. I awoke in this state, but to be awake through it must be quite awful. I have never seen its early stages but its middle stages involve losing all ability to communicate in any effective way, along with deadening of the limbs, the heart stopping beating, the mind shutting down due to internal bleeding, cognition becom-ing an ailment and the blood in your veins freezing. Its causes vary from person to person.

The woman across from me is dying. I can see the hope she had in her eyes earlier is fading rapidly; her family visited her earlier but she wasn't all there and they cried a little. They left her a bunch of flowers carefully arranged in a vase and she ate them. The nurse had to pull them from her wrinkled, clutching hands. Yellow and white carnations, they were. Nobody will come to visit me and I am glad. My friends and family haven't seen a zombie before.

The radio is playing and the sound drowns me so I fall back asleep, seeing Mia and Mel seated in the hospital cafeteria waiting for me; but I am in a fixed position that I can't move. I cannot even try at the minute. When I awake a nurse is wiping the dribble from my mouth. She sits me up properly, arranging my pillows but it's not how I want them. I can speak a little now so I ask her, "How long will I be on this drip?" She says it has another four or five hours left. The buzzing noise it is making is disheartening. I look at my arms again and they feel bruised, the blue tinge set on them.

I think, I think and I think some more, even though it hurts my head to do so. I realise through memories of yesterday that I did this to myself; it is not the drip as I thought. Can I live being a zombie? Can I find a cure?

As the nurse goes to make me a cup of tea, I sit up to see the lady opposite is drinking milk from a baby's bottle and the woman in the bed at my side has a 'gone out' stare on her wizened face. Is she dead? I blink a few times but she doesn't move, not even to blink. So I muster all my strength to turn onto my side away from her, feeling sharp pains hit my hips and along my legs. Has my muscle turned to dust? Am I just bone now? This idea doesn't bear thinking about. The nurse returns with my tea and says, "You need to try and sit up. You will make the pain worse if you just remain still." She is a sadist so I don't move and I don't answer, I just let salty tears trickle down my face; this comforts me greatly because it means I have not been taken over completely by this sickness yet.

A nurse wheels round across the squeaky clean floor with the heart rate monitor. I start to feel sick with the hospital smell. The woman in the bed next to me has moved her position and I am relieved she is not dead. I don't like the idea of lying in the same room just metres away from death. The nurse wraps the cuff around my upper arm and it squeezes tightly, trying to get a reading, and although I feel no beat the nurse writes something down and looks up positively.

"Yep, that's fine, a little on the low side but nothing to worry about."

"Thanks," I croak, nodding.

I am going to mentally fight against this potentially fatal illness; I am going to beat it. I will never piss myself or eat flowers, just as I will never amount to anything great, but I am past caring. I can handle just being a normal person. All I know right now is that I don't want to become a full-blown zombie; I might be transitioning into one but I can reverse the depression, I can make it back to a normal state. I can and I can't, but I must try.

"You're not having me," I say to the sickness, and begin with standing still inside. I make myself tranquil and picture myself on a beach, surrounded by friends and family and people who are full of life, so I picture myself full of life. We are sipping cocktails and my body is healthy, very healthy, my skin is glowing, I see my little sister - she is thirteen years old now and her name is Faye and she needs me, and her sweet smile is enough to keep my head on this imaginary beach for a short while. She is all happiness and daisy chains. She is music and life and she is still here.

I see Kim as a ghost, drinking champagne in Heaven, and she tells me to fight and keep going; she sprinkles down angel dust from the clouds onto me and the others on the white beach and we all smile with our eyes. We have soft eyes and flowing dresses that the wind lifts as we twirl. I am a part of their future. I am not a vegetable, not gloomy, I am happy and finding my happiness through their happiness. My angel sister, Kim, is telling me that the only cure to this zombie sickness, the only way to reverse it, is to sit and count my blessings. So I come back from the imaginary beach, telling everyone I will see them soon, then I press the buzzer and the nurse rushes in.

"I need something. I need a piece of scrap paper and a pen, please."

"Okay, love." She looks pleased that I am talking, brings me a pen and a piece of paper, and I sit and write all my blessings down and as I do so the mind sickness lifts. I do this over the next few hours. I eat some food, actually feeding myself, and say Grace in my head; I also feel bad about all the food I have purged in the past, but I was heavy with anxiety, so I make an apology to an imaginary Creator and this makes me feel good.

The woman across from me is deteriorating. I feel a tinge of guilt for fighting this when she cannot, but I have to. I go to sleep, thinking sleep will revive me a little more and it works wonders because as I awaken a doctor is taking the drip out.

"How are you feeling?" he asks.

"I don't know," I answer bluntly. I clench my fist then release and so on in four-second intervals to keep the blood flowing, just in case I haven't reversed the sickness. Just in case I have already ripped apart all my blessings through suicide notes.

"Okay, well, we just need to take some more bloods and get your results back. If everything is good, you can be on your way tomorrow morning. I've phoned the mental health crisis team and if you're happy with them coming to see you at home then I'll arrange that. To your aunt's and uncle's house?"

I nod. I have made it.

"Well, I'll send the nurse to do your bloods now and 'phone the crisis team to arrange a visit."

I nod a second time. He walks away. The nurses take my bloods.

From now on I just need to focus on keeping sickness away when I get out of here. I will never be a zombie because being a zombie would suck. And the women on the ward with me have nearly fully transformed; one is sent to Fieldhead hospital and I feel sympathy for her. The other is sent to a different ward. The woman who has gone to Fieldhead has a higher chance of recovery than the other one. And because I am still young, I have a higher chance of recovery than people who have fought against this illness all their lives. Eventually it will take a few of them and that will be the end of them.

I go to the hospital chapel, though it takes me a while to get there because I have to take slow steps and I have to walk at the pace elderly people do. I also have to hold the back of my gown scrunched onto my side so as not to show my arse to Pinder-fields. I never did understand why hospitals dress people in gowns that reveal their backsides.

I make it there and I light a candle for all those suffering from mind sickness, then light another candle for my dead sister and all the people who are still in this life and who I am blessed to have in my life.

This was one of the many times I have been in hospital after an overdose, and it did lead to Fieldhead.

SIX

CLARENCE MUSIC FESTIVAL

My Dad comes to see me with his girlfriend; they have visited a few times this week and I have done nothing but talk of the other patients to them. I have tried to sit down but failed because I have been constantly on the lookout for Tobias. They are glad I am making friends. Today I have nothing planned and I have spent the morning entertaining Carl.

Carl is a patient who you can clearly tell is a patient, unlike Adam and Liz who appear normal - a word I hate to use because normal people are crazier than crazy people, but normal in the sense that they talk without the incoherent sentences of a schizophrenic like Carl. Carl told me he has given me the 'Power of Destiny' and I went along with this because I found I can only connect with him if I bring myself hypothetically into his world. His world consists of a crew whom he rescued from the raging fires of Hell. Now, on the crew there is a unicorn called Chief, a monster called Clever Monster, a cat called Pearl Essence and a Spider Boy. They are his friends and who can take them away from him? They are real to him and who is to say what's real and what's not?

Reality is subjective. Staff members say I should not entertain his delusional ideas; but staff also tell me it is a sin to make friends on the ward. Some staff also have their heads stuck up their arses so I will not be taking their advice on board anytime soon.

A nurse came and knocked on the door, poking her head around it. Her hair is white and she appeared motherly when I first met her. After she witnessed my first outburst of emotion, though, she scolded me and withdrew her motherly words because emotion is not something one is allowed simply to express in the adult world - it must be contained until there's a suitable environment for outlet.

"Elisa, your Dad and his girlfriend are here to see you," she said, then looked at Carl who was seated in the middle of the floor scribbling a picture of Clever Monster. He appeared like a little boy trapped in a world of make-believe. I enjoy watching him like this as it is very endearing.

"Okay," I said, standing.

Carl looked up at me. "You're not leaving, are you?"

"No, but I am allowed out now for three hours so I'm going to go out with my Dad and his girlfriend," I said. "Here's my number so text me if you like, Carl." I knew I was being defiant because the once motherly nurse gave me a disapproving glance.

"Thanks," he said and smiled, revealing teeth that suggest a previous drug habit.

"Have a nice day, Carl," I said, and as I left I felt so bad for him. He has been here for one and a half years. He was on the ward next door, Trinity, but was then moved into here; he told me he'd tried to stab himself after his lover left him. He is now only allowed out for fifteen minutes and this is escorted leave, when the staff can manage to pull themselves away from their desks.

I walk over to my Dad and Sandra. I am gleeful and ignore my inner voice telling me not to hug my Dad because hugs are weird and I didn't even used to hug Kim, so I hug him tightly and he smiles and I am happy he is pleased to see me because I was beginning to wonder if I still existed outside these hospital walls. I remind them that I am dying to get out of this ward, which is a lie and we all know it.

One of the days they came up, Sandra got talking to another patient that she knew from The Talbot, an Irish pub in town. My Dad lives in a room above it and me and Kim when we first met him used to spend time in this room in this Irish pub, full of character. As we got to know our Dad, we found many traits we had in common with him, particularly our dry sense of humour.

"Lace Head, we're going to take you out," my Dad says, "if that's okay with you," he adds, looking into the staff office. A female member who is seated at a desk spins around on her chair with her mouth half full and answers, "Yes, that's fine, she's got three hours." She then gets up and looks a little flustered, probably because she has dead legs from sitting in the same position for hours. She writes my name down on the white board and I turn to my Dad and roll my eyes because this all feels very formal.

My Dad met Otak a few times and disliked him (my Dad has good intuition). My Mum never met him and this was because I was not going to have evil in my Mum's house; I put obstacles in the way when it came to that because my Mum would have liked him. She wouldn't have picked up on his sinister eyes or the way I was being treated badly for a second time round. Or maybe I was scared of her picking up on it but being helpless. The 'eyes of a madman' was definitely applicable to Otak. However, being stupid, I didn't pick up on his sociopathic eyes until they looked into mine for the first time and told me, "I am going to kill you so stay quiet." This occurrence became commonplace. And I must admit that when I first saw a huge kitchen knife in his hands, as he told me to be quiet, so he could kill me much faster and easier, I was petrified.

"Come on, Lacey," Sandra says as a nurse stands up to buzz us out.

Sandra has a mullet and wears kids' trainers and a leather jacket; my Dad often wears trainers, jeans and random tee shirts. He always has a rucksack on his back too because he sells DVDs and makes a living doing this. He sits in different pubs around Wakefield and everybody knows him as DVD Paul. When I first met him I was seventeen; Kim wasn't there because she was in her own flat that Social Services had placed her in, in Wales. She told me to wait for her before I went to meet him so we could meet him together, but I've always found patience to be anything but a virtue.

Tobias is at the other side of the automatic doors and my heart skips a beat as they open. I freeze and stare and he is bedraggled and bonnie. His eyes say all the words he cannot verbally articulate so well.

"Come on, Lacey," Sandra says, disturbing the intensity of the moment. I pause as he passes, turn from my Dad and Sandra and run over to him as they exit through the doors.

"Tobias!" I shout and he turns around. I stutter, "D… do you want some cigs?" and pull five out of my packet of Benson and Hedges Silver.

"Yes, please," he says and takes them from my hand. I offer him cigs because he smokes an awful lot and often runs out so has to ask me for more. Others shun him and tell me not to give him cigarettes because he has plenty of money and can get his own. I save baccy from my Dad and have it ready to give Tobias when he asks, and when he does it is the highlight of my day; and although very briefly, I feel okay and young again (I am still young but I often do not feel it).

"I'm coming," I say, feeling silly because Sandra is looking at me as if I am mad. My Dad just smiles and shakes his head.

"Where are we going?" I ask as we stand at the entrance to Priory 2. Sandra pulls her `phone out and orders a taxi and I wonder how she is not sweltering in the jacket she is wearing.

"We're going to Clarence, David is there," my Dad says.

I love my brother but I don't know him all that well and over the past year I have not had much chance to try to get to know him. The week prior to the doll transition, my brother came over to see Kim. We were sat on a bench outside McDonalds and Otak had been following us both around town as we entered various charity shops, trying to be two normal sisters, picking up bits and bobs, laughing to gloss over the anxiety within because we knew we were going to have to build up our bond again. In the air was a scent of separation that needed dissolving.

When my brother approached us, I had a rose in my hand and a spider in my throat as he walked over to the benches. I couldn't speak, I didn't even look at him because I was seated next to Otak and didn't want to trigger any more of his false tears as he said, "Please come back, I'll change." Kim just sat on the opposite bench growing bored and biting her nails that were always thick with clumpy nail varnish, usually glittery. I look at Sandra's nails and they're clumpy too, so I push my shades further up the bridge of my nose.

"Ah, okay… Can't really remember Clarence beyond childhood."

Clarence is a small town music festival. It's really an excuse for a load of people to sit on a hill and get as pissed as they can. But I can remember kite-making there with Kim when we were young.

I wish I didn't have to hand over my thoughts and memories of Kim to some unseen force to live, but I do because continuing to live and loving her are contradictory and contradictions muddle my head. Suicide and loving Kim go hand in hand. But now, nobody is telling me how I should be acting. After the death of a loved one, months after, one might wonder if it is okay to go out and smile. And how long should one wait before they can go out and live? Even the basics of living are neglected because when neglected they are proof to the dead that one is committed to a relationship that will never see the light again.

My Dad is slightly drunk so is taking the piss out of the taxi driver who has limited English; I don't like the taxi driver when he talks either because he reminds me of Otak, whose English was also limited and baby-like. Me and Kim mocked his accent a week before the event as we sat in her new flat in Wakefield.

"I can't even pronounce his name properly," I said,

"You have to emphasise the 'k'," she replied.

"But there's no 'k' in Ahmad," I said, shrugging my shoulders.

We both burst out laughing as we made exaggerated impressions of how people pronounced his name. I saw a light in Kim's eyes that night as we joked and I knew that she had been in the dark for so long like me. We attracted bad boyfriends so well and we even briefly joked about how when a guy was angry and violent it made us laugh completely out of nerves.

"You seem very dreamy today," Sandra says.

"Yeah, lack of sleep," I reply.

"Let's just get into the park. David's waiting and I want to sit down," my Dad says.

In my head I am debating whether I should be a rule-breaker and drink. I shouldn't because it is against the rules to return to the ward under the influence of alcohol. I debate for a matter of seconds and decide I don't care about the rules. I never want to become one of those people who forget how to live, people who have had something bad or tragic happen to them and live the rest of their lives in despair. Some people just forget how to have fun, not because anything bad has happened to them but because they get caught up in life, in work, in expectations and in adulthood. I swear I will never become one of those people. I would rather hang.

"Can we get some booze?" I say, as I text a friend inviting her to turn up here.

"Y'sure that's what ya wanting?" Sandra says, pulling her purse out.

"No, no, I'll get it," I say.

"Lace Head, what do you want?" my Dad says, smiling.

"Malibu and lemonade."

"I'll get this and it's just for you, ya Dad's got some cans in his bag and a small bottle of vodka," Sandra says.

"Yeah, and Mary and Malcom are gonna be there, and George, and they've all got a couple of crates." My Dad's friends are comical and also drunks but the nice kind. His friend George looks like the lion from the Wizard of Oz. My brother will also have some alcohol I presume and although I am a cheap drunk and become tipsy very easily, I like to make sure I have enough alcohol to cover me. If you are going to drink then might as well do it in style. Yes, my idea of style is getting intoxicated, with either alcohol or notions of love.

We sit down and we drink and we laugh and I feel fine and with each sip I take I become more relaxed in myself. The yellow sun in the sky is a ball of hope. I sit with my friend Natalie; she was mine and Kim's best friend for a while. We didn't often like any other female company besides each other's until we met Natalie when we were in our early teens, before we ended up in care. We were all rogues, just lost, wild youths that had taken things too far. None of us attended school; we loved boys in fast cars, drugs, alcohol and shoplifting.

As I sit, the music pounds through me. Clarence is held in Thorne's Park on a big hill with a bandstand at the bottom. The music is metal and the bands that are currently playing are not the kind of metal I usually like; they have long messy hair and appear to be in their forties. The hill is a disarray of metal heads and chavs with cans in their hands.

I decide I am impartial to the dress code of others. The art of not caring can be pretty useful, a new trait I have just assigned to myself, and maybe it is this that's leading me to drop all defences and go into the bushes with a group of chavs to snort white powder up my nose. And as the sky darkens I realise that my Dad and his girlfriend are nowhere to be seen.

"Where's David?" I ask Natalie.

"He went off to a house party," she slurs.

I nearly stumble so I grasp hold of a chav guy who steadies me. I somehow end up kissing him and although he makes me feel sick I enjoy it because I close my eyes and realise I am starved of affection.

"Okay, when you're finished," Natalie says and walks towards the group of five or six guys and two girls. I pull myself away from the guy and walk towards Natalie.

"I gotta get back," I say, realising that I have no way to get home and I lost my money.

"Where do you live?" a chav girl with honeycomb hair asks.

"In Fieldhead," I say. They all laugh and I don't care because I've let go of people's thoughts about me. This is what freedom is about, I think.

"I'm going with these," Natalie says, pointing to a couple of guys in track suits. They are people Kim used to know and I am not fond of them, so when two random girls ask me if I want to hit some clubs with them I agree on impulse. I agree because I want to go and be a slut. This sounds dumb and Kim was often accused of being a slut whereas I am often accused of being frigid. But not now, I want to experience a one night stand. I want someone to put their hands all over me as I seductively dance and make them want me more than they have ever wanted anyone, just because I can.

So me and the two girls walk on to Westgate, where all the clubs are dotted. From the bottom of Westgate to the top, people outside engage in drunken banter. Women with sparkly eyes make me wish I were a little less me and a little more sparkly. I have never been into a club before besides one that me and Kim used to sneak into when I was fifteen and back then we wore slightly too dark foundation and large hooped earrings. All three of us dance and I feel unsteady but I don't stop. I jump onto a ledge and begin dancing with a guy who is not my type and I see two of him; he puts his hands down my shorts and I try not to push him off me, then we move from club to club and as the music infiltrates my mind I begin kissing one of the girls. And I like it. We finish kissing and I go to pick my drink up, then I look down to her chest and she has a knife stuck into her; she pulls it out and licks the blood off it slowly, her exotic-looking hair covering the wound, and she looks all sarcastic as she talks.

"What's the matter?"

I look around me and everyone's faces are like dark clowns. They are moving out of time and don't notice the girl with her knife; she lifts her top up and puts the knife in her distressed denim shorts waistline. I take a deep breath and all of a sudden I am back in reality and the girl is shaking me.

"You didn't enjoy that kiss did you?" she says, handing me and the other girl a shot of tequila.

I look around and wish I had Kim to come and pull me out of this white noise that I'm currently experiencing. I try to start a conversation with a guy who is dancing with me but he doesn't really respond. I want to strangle him and watch his body convulse as he begs for forgiveness for being too drunk to treat a girl with respect. The time is 1 a.m. As we step out onto the pavement I realise that I'm alone outside a nightclub and I hope my vulnerability gets me murdered; this is not a good thing to think, but it is what I think. A policeman walks by and my Uncle Arthur walks over the road. I am shocked.

"Shit, my uncle is there," I say. When I look around, the two girls are walking away. The policeman asks me my name so I tell him honestly. Muffled words vibrate through his radio and hurt my ears.

"My name's Elisa Frank and I'm missing from Fieldhead," I say to the officer. He gets onto his radio.

"What are you doing? We've been worried," my uncle says, looking back and forth between me and the officer with a confused face.

"Like fuck you were worried," I mutter, getting out of the high heels that have crippled my feet. The olive-skinned girl has a good taste in shoes but heels are not my thing and I've left her with my flats. My blistered feet don't touch the ground from the bus stop bench where I'm sitting now because I am only five foot three. I kick my bare feet back and forth as the officer and my uncle talk briefly. The blisters look swollen and painful.

"Come on then, love," the officer, says so I walk to the car and say goodbye to nightlife and its promiscuity and sin.

The policeman kindly hands me over to the Priory 2 night staff who make me a cup of tea and send me to bed where I throw up in my bin as Mel kindly holds my hair back. I then fall asleep, for the first night without Zopiclone's helping hand.

I awake and text my Dad to see where he and Sandra ended up. Apparently my Dad went rolling down Thorne's Hill and ended up being strapped into an ambulance. Typical and funny, Kim would have loved that.

Of course, I am grounded, meaning that the doctor tells the nurses I am not allowed off the ward for a week, so I spend a week perving on Tobias and reading Alice's Adventures in

Wonderland. I am in wonderland here. Carl gives me a Cheshire Cat grin and I play the role of Alice, and when we all dine we should be given a teapot (and probably a line of medication too) but we'd all play the Mad Hatter's tea party scene perfectly. And Kim will laugh from cloud nine, or ten, wherever she is, cheering me on, because Heaven is probably a boring place for young people.

SEVEN

A WAKING DREAM

A waking dream, a waking awareness,
a surrealist heart, I can, I can't,
a trance that leads me to depart
from the world that you call home.
I can't make it all alone,
to slumber I surrender,
I can't make it through December…
A waking whirlwind of angel dust,
I give in too easily to love and lust,
answers automatic and artless talk
as in reality through dreams I walk.

My dreams keep merging and mixing into my daily waking life. I sit and write my diary in the small women's lounge because my diary is very understanding and I can't explain what I mean verbally. I am contemplating my whole self. 'Emotionally unstable personality disorder' – I'm reading a leaflet I picked up from the hospital cafe this morning, because the doctor has diagnosed me. I discussed with Mel the possibility of the doctor being an imposter and Mel said

I should confront him. I said it doesn't matter, I'll let it slide and pretend I don't know. I wouldn't want to embarrass the poor man.

It is a profound moment when you realise you have established yourself as a loon. When you realise you have accidently trodden too far from all you once knew and maybe have accidently left people behind. Or maybe they abandoned you when they realised you no longer made sense to them. But you don't ever want to go back to your old regular routine when you step into the light of insanity. In these asylum corridors, the white walls can hold people's originality and outlandish utterances, in fact hysterical laughter goes over people's heads and nobody looks at you if you suddenly decide to take a rock from the courtyard and try to eat it or if you want to talk to your imaginary friends while sitting right next to another patient. If you should decide you want to dance in rapture or `phone the Fire Brigade and demand attention (or you will blow your head off), all of these behaviours are okay. I tried the latter. Patients build rapport with each other because of similar peculiarities in character. Similar, but no two people are ever the same.

The doctor has noted that my behaviours are both 'risky' and 'inappropriate' as far as my interactions with male patients are concerned. This is not factual. I am a very flirty, playful character, but I treat male and female exactly the same. Our spirits have no gender, see; either that or we are both genders in spirit.

The doctor believes that I am overly provocative because he is gullible. I cried when he asked me if I had tried kissing another patient, who is currently spending a lot of time with me; I cried and the doctor looked at the nurses, who looked at my social worker, and they offered no words of comfort and ignored my spoken rejections of such a ridiculous question. I did not try to kiss the patient they had suggested. I did, however, kiss Tobias but let's just keep that between me and you.

Did Kim fall into a dream within a dream? I begin to write and when I start I do not stop...

> Did she fall into a dream within a dream? Maybe she fell into a scene within a scene? If you fall into a dream within a dream endlessly it must be terribly hard to return from. Maybe the further you get into dreams within dreams, the further you are from reality. This seems blissful and, for dream ghosts, a release. My sister is a dream ghost. This means she is not real anymore in any other sense than how my subconscious mind makes her - in my dreams or other people's dreams. In my dreams she tells me she is sick to death of being a dream ghost, sick to death of acting out her turmoil night after night. I tell her she must stay awake and never let her head hit a pillow in my dream world, for if she does she will have fallen into a dream within a dream and won't ever make it back to me. If her head hits a pillow it will be like her head hitting concrete and shattering her skull, which will be shards of bone in my trembling distorted dreamer's hands.
>
> She tells me one day that this is imminent. I tell her not any time soon because I'm selfish and I like her company in dreamland. I miss the way we were dreamers once. Me and her. We are still dreamers though because dreaming is all I can do; sometimes this beats reality because we cannot fly through summery skies in reality. As it is, summery skies are ours to fall through 'til we hit a meadow with animated flowers that we would sink into laughing. Appreciating summer.

I have been spending my mornings arranging a graceful demeanour for myself due to the fact I have been in Tobias' presence. Yesterday morning we had been discussing the hidden meanings in the film Donnie Darko; the discussion didn't last long because he is very reserved in his opinions and also because my Mum decided to pay me a visit. The nurses spoke to her on the `phone a few days ago and told her it may be beneficial for us both if she came to see me. After all, I am still her daughter (much to her dismay).

We cried when we sat down together in the visiting room. I'd forgotten that I loved my Mum until this moment. And I was thankful that she did not bring my little sister. Faye balled her eyes out at the funeral and all I wanted to do was run out of the church and scream, "Where the fuck are you, Kim?" because my heart twisted and turned as Faye's sobs became louder and my Mum squeezed my hand tighter and tighter in the front pew where we were seated. The vicar made religious ramblings and references. The whole of the church was etched with tragedy, for young people do not simply die. Oh, but apparently they do, they really do, my heart said as I stood up to read a poem with a shaky voice...

I left a note for Tobias earlier although I suspect he cannot read, but I did so hoping he would pick up on the fact the note is more to offer friendship when we get out of here and maybe even get better. We have established an unspoken bond already through our mutual dedication to picking out the darker elements of life. I told my blue-eyed doctor about this and he waved his hand saying, "It's normal to have crushes on guys." I saw this comment as an insult because I am not one who merely 'crushes' on another, I am far too deep for something so unsubstantial and unpromising.

I hope Tobias reads my note. I am no good with words that are spoken so I write them down. If I had to speak half of the things I have told you so far, I'd be here for the next hundred years and my throat would never produce the right sounding words. My words often come out devoid of emotion; this is not because the emotion is not there but because this is just how I speak. Mel is good with words; he is very good with words actually. At the funeral Mel stood by my side, on my left because my mother and Faye were on the right. He also helped me prepare for the funeral and I rehearsed the poem I was going to read out to him about a hundred times in my room at my aunt's and uncle's.

I stretch out my arms and let out a long yawn. The evening is beginning to take its toll and I'm growing tired, drinking a caramel latte which I picked up from Pinderfields Hospital shop while out with my Dad and his girlfriend earlier. It's weird, you know, when you realise that you like your own father, when you realise you love your parents. See, I never knew before, I never knew I loved my mother; I guess that may seem weird but it really is true that you don't know what you have until it's gone. I still have my mother, of course, but only to a certain extent; we are connected yet we are so very separate. My Dad is a different story because he is jokes and inspiration and we write together now and we share poetry. Although it hasn't always been this way.

I look at Mel now and I feel my love for him is a replace-ment for the love I had for my sister; I had to direct it into something - something beautiful - and Mel is just that. If I didn't direct my love for my sister somewhere I may become bitter or I fear it would dissolve just like my memory will one day.

Tobias told me he had not read my note. I felt a little hurt but just as he has dyslexia I have emotional dyslexia and anorexia, so the prognosis for me forming relationships is rather grim. I would have to go through several years' therapy first. I don't want therapy. I like my style of loving another, even though it is completely fucked up. I will never love anyone else in the unconditional manner that I did Kim.

"You look deep in thought," Mel says, closing his collage book.

"Mel, how long do you think I can hang on to you for?" I ask sincerely.

"Well, that all depends on you," he says, shrugging his shoulders. Mel never goes too far into detail when responding to my questions. He doesn't do this purposely but because revelations that are worth clinging onto have to be made all by oneself. He says so, anyway.

"Do you think I will let you go one day?" I ask.

"No, not as long as you remember to include me in your work, as long as I am in here," he says, pointing to his head.

"I guess so. It's just… I don't know," I sigh, and when I hear a nightingale sing from where it is perched on the tree next to my window I crave to fall into my city of possibilities, where the sky jets and the heavy sedation begins. I am quickly learning to dream lucidly. My favourite part of my dreams is when I am falling through velvety skies and I shut my eyes and pray to hit the concrete ground… and splat, my body would be a work of art. Although gruesome, it would certainly be a statement.

Currently Mel is sat creating a collage. He went out earlier and caught butterflies, or 'beautiful moths' as he calls them (he likes word combinations that merge beauty with ugliness). He caught white ones and pink ones and Blue Morphos too. Blue Morphos are brilliant, their blue wings vivid. Mel has dried them out and now he wants to sellotape them to the thick cream collage pages. He knows that I will probably lose this collage book, for I can never hang onto anything for longer than a few months, but I like his enthusiasm towards wrecking dainty things such as butterflies' wings. This reminds me of a poem

Mel wrote, for which he had used his best fountain pen to write out in the collage book. I stored it in a file held secretly in my mind.

ALEXIS

Alexis, with azurite eyes,
deep, right to the ocean floor,
emotionally obscure
nevertheless my cure

I recall her micro-expressions
as she folds butterflies' wings
several times, like origami,
and she does not want me,
she's too full of rosy notions

Deathly devoted to dissection,
obsessing of her reflection,
perfecting dreamlike features
of herself, and other creatures

She thrills in this,
yes, she gets her kicks, and kills,
watching the embers of dainty daisies
she set alight last night, in spite,
with all the notes I write

Mesmerised, I watch
as Alexis feebly threads
a butterfly's wings
to an earthworm's head

She whispers her sweet sanity,
self-declared, into sea shells
and my heart swells
at her simple, smouldering beauty
the thread, the dread
of the frayed thread, that leads
our hearts to one another,
a phase, in long lost days,
yes, she is my phase,
Alexis with azurite gaze

This poem is now mentally locked away for the rest of my days, we all need some form of words to hang on to, not just regular words that we hear often but beautiful words, unique words, whether they be spoken to us by a friend, the quote of an inspirational leader or words we have spoken or written ourselves whilst channelling our wiser selves. Kim's were "Fuck it", and that's perfect in any situation. I hang on to every word I hear that comes out of Mel's mind; now he is looking at me as though mildly confused, his face the golden ratio and his eyes identical to Tobias's.

It's 2.15 a.m. and I awake abruptly. I am paralysed. I am petrified. Alexis is here on top of my chest, her small hands wrapped tightly around my throat... I try to move but cannot as I feel her grip grow tighter and tighter and my head becomes lighter and lighter. I should have mentioned that Alexis is Mel's ex-lover. She is brilliant white and the contours of her face are sharp and shadowed.

Alexis is a banshee, a revenge seeker. Mel left her broken and forlorn and she turned bitter, crying tears of acid. Her heart grew so cold that it turned to ice and then melted inside her chest. She killed herself at this point. She spent many months begging for Mel to return but he left her for me. She told her therapist for months and months of her chest problems and broken heart. She told her mother she was going to die. And then she did, jumping from a seven-storey car park in the middle of the city centre. When she did this, death gave her the gift of becoming a banshee and she swore she would hunt Mel down and kill any future lover of his.

Now she is really going for it, her azurite eyes full of pleasure as I begin gasping for air and failing to shriek. The contrast of her raven hair against her white ghoul-like face is stunning. She lets out a wail and I wonder, 'Can this really be the end of me?' I pray to a God who hates me as Alexis lets out crazy laughs that rattle through my ears and the halls of insanity, echoing hidden truths into patients' bedrooms. But no-one will come for me, the night staff are oblivious to everything and anything. I am fading and the blackness that surrounds me is caving in on me. I cannot die, though. Trust me when I say I am invincible. I survived many life-threatening situations in my time and I sail right through them untouched. I don't know why this is so and I am not bragging. It just appears that 'someone up there' - or 'down there' - loves me. Or maybe it's Mel who looks after me.

Alexis thinks she has ended me. I lie there and close my eyes, pretending to be dead. She doesn't move, though she does apologise with her child-like voice over and over. Mel walks in. He's good at being a holy saviour. He walks in and when I open my eyes he grabs Alexis by her tiny waist that is pulled in by a white corset and she breaks into hysterics.

"You're not dead!" she screams at me.

"Fuck you, bitch!" I scream back, but Mel tells me to shut up. So I watch her fall apart on my bedroom floor and now I know what Mel meant when he said she was a fruitcake. I wish there was opportunities for dead girls to receive therapy, or medication if needs be. Alexis needs a straightjacket too. Mel said last week that she had been stalking him. Her cries and wails are getting louder and more painful. Her throat is sore and

I wonder how Mel has patience with her, as I sit with my legs against my chest.

"Alexis, sweetie, you can't go on this way," Mel says, as she directs her anger towards herself, slashing at her wrists and getting blood all over my bedroom floor.

"I hate you! I can do what I want!" she screeches.

"You can't try to kill my friends, though!" he yells back.

"Why did you leave me?" She breaks into sobs and it dawns on me that she is not a bad person. She is not evil, slightly disturbed, yes, but she just needs a little bit of help.

Mel is standing and I can barely see his face, so do not know his expression, while Alexis is on the floor looking up at him and slowly becoming silent. When she is calmer he sits down and lifts her head, tilts her chin towards him and holds her heart-shaped face in his hands. She just looks at me and now I am speechless, I don't know what to say, and they don't know what to say to each other either; so we all fall still and remain this way for a while. Alexis begins yawning and I throw them both a pillow so they can put their heads down. The wind lets itself in through my window and sings a lullaby as it blows rings around the glasses on my bedside table. I hear Alexis singing too and Mel doing a bit of hypnosis on her. When I awake I ask Mel where she is.

"She is gone now," he says, matter of fact.

"Gone where?" I ask, puzzled.

"She fell asleep, so now she's in a dream within a dream."

"Ah, I am so sorry," I say, realising that I dreamed Alexis up. I wish my sister would fall into this dream within a dream sometimes, because I am sick of seeing her bloody. If I never saw her again, if she fell into a dream within a dream and dined with Edgar Allen Poe, I would be both happy and sad. I have forgotten what her voice sounds like. I can only remember her voice if she stays within my dreams and doesn't fall asleep in them quite yet. But one fine day, maybe I will allow her to do so.

EIGHT

THE MAGIC CARPET

Right now I am unsure about anything other than that I have a desire to bathe in soothing cocoa bath oil and listen to the chit chat of the cleaning staff in the corridors. I don't usually take a bath in the morning but I feel that if I lie there then I will come up with a plan for the day. I take my hospital towel and ask for the bathroom to be opened, hoping to dissolve in the milky water; the oil makes my skin feel silken soft. I approve, putting my head back ready to listen to my inner self come up with an adventure for the day. I listen to footsteps as I sit up swishing the water with my hands. The sound is that of patients walking round to the medical room for morning medication. I am on nothing on mornings so I stay where I am as time passes and the water turns cold. I pull myself out of the bath and tiptoe across to the towel rail so I don't get water everywhere, wrapping the towel around my bust as I prepare to brush my teeth. I am refreshed, so why do I look so blemished?

I brush my thinning teeth at least seven times a day now. The enamel has been eroded by my stomach acid when I throw up. Over-brushing is not good, I am told, but I don't care if my gums bleed a little; I relish any pain and the feeling of bleeding gums is kind of pleasurable. It's become a kind of habit that began in here, the same as my cigarette consumption which has grew considerably to about twenty a day. My throat hurts and to be honest by the time I leave here I will probably be going round the corner to the general hospital for smoking-related problems.

I walk into the dining hall with a spring in my step. These walls of peaceful, bland blue won't get me down because today I am allowed out for a couple of hours. And not just on the hospital grounds, which by the way happen to be quite large with a café situated at the top end next to a building where all the criminally insane are put. I see them in the Oasis Café sometimes, where they are always escorted and always very polite in speech. The café is run by a woman who could easily pass as a patient, smiley and rather round. Good for her, I think, as smiley people are liked right away, especially the chubby kind, although overly smiley people are just seen as weird because it's like they know something you don't.

The other patients are just finishing breakfast. I say "Hello" to Adam and Carla, who still has jam around her mouth, and ask for a clean cup as all the other pastel blue plastic cups have been taken.

"You up for a game of pool?" Ron shouts from the pool table. He has shaved his beard off to impress me, I gather. A few days ago, Jess told me that he fancies me but I told her I dislike facial hair.

"Maybe later," I say, taking the cup from a young girl serving. I walk over to the trolley and pour my coffee out of the heavy, black plastic jug. All cutlery here is plastic too, well, for that matter everything here is; it is a sugar-coated world built out of plastic and does not resemble the real world in any sense. It's a bubble for us all to float around in and try to get 'better', whatever that means.

I perch myself by the window and watch Ron hitting the balls with precision; he looks rather dashing without a beard but I was put off him a few days ago when he ate his cereal and was told off by a member of the nursing staff (who sit observing in the corner during meals) for pouring sugar from other people's tables in piles onto his Weetabix. "Ron, you'll get worms if you eat like that," they said. So from that moment on, I associated Ron with worms. And beards.

Polishing off my coffee – decaffeinated, not by choice - I am refreshed and eager to get out and about. I ask the staff to mark me out until 12.30 p.m. as its 9.30 a.m. currently, so they squeak the marker across the whiteboard next to the office door. The nurse who lets me out is nice and compliments me on my pastel pink cherry dress. She is a motherly figure, if you know what I mean. I have had a few of those throughout my life; my old Connexions worker was like this in some ways, like an owl, wise. I told her she wasn't the barn kind but a snowy, full of wisdom that was worded in a way you took it in. A down-to-earth character. I still remember much of what I learned from her during four years and I still think of what she would say at times when I need advice. She gave me a wishes jar and I will complete each of my dreams; small as they are, they are mine and they mean something to me so I promised her I would complete them. Although promises mean Jack Shit, I am not one to go back on them if they are of personal importance.

I take my satchel with me everywhere I go, with my butterfly journal inside to record people and places that I find interesting. I have always recorded events in my life, usually in the form of poetry, though now I like to describe events and record my observations, my own thoughts and notions. Sometimes I worry that I will become so involved in writing about life that I may forget to live it. I walk through the hospital grounds and the yellow of the daffodils is a colour of vitality to me; these flowers appeal to me because they are not spectacular but are just, well, cheery. If they could talk, I imagine they would be like children and sing and laugh.

I board the bus and at last reach the city centre after enduring a terrible journey. Buses make me feel sick and people don't seem to talk much on the bus amongst each other, yet I become overwhelmed with the chatter. The city centre has a cathedral which is very beautiful inside, something I don't like to admit because Wakefield is not my favourite place and I've always thought that people in Wakefield never become amazing people; they are the kind of people whose stories are always very clichéd and only appeal to the boring kind of mind. Average and tedious, neither in a bad way nor a good one. I could be wrong, though.

If you ever want to sit and people-watch, a coffee shop is Heaven. People around are all different and unique in the way they talk and the way they dress, and sometimes their little conversations make me smile inside. So when I sit down with my coffee I expect nothing and hope my pen will do the magic, twisting and turning a somewhat ordinary day into a day of whimsical beings, disguising the fact that the figures in this place are not mere coffee shop people but magicians in training. The girls my age are not just students full of hope to gain their degrees in various subjects, which will lead to full-time jobs whilst also giving them something to talk about when they meet each other, but privately they know the secrets of the universe and how to define beauty without owning it for themselves. But I can't do this for everyone I see because then magnificence would become ordinary. And I don't want to spoil the world, or make others out to be better than me or better than Kim. It would be pretty hard to become better than a dead girl who died in that way and impossible to beat her fiery personality; she was the kind of character who, like Sammy, gave you a natural high when in their company.

I sit with a newspaper on my lap. I like to scan it and pretend I am reading it, with my journal on the table and my pen ready, always ready. I sip my soya latte and the newspaper print makes my head hurt, so I lift my gaze to a table in front of me where there's a young man with auburn hair and flawed skin, looking rather meditative in thought.

He looks like a genie, so I label him a hippy and begin from there, entitling this chapter in my journal 'The Magic Carpet'. I imagine that in his rucksack he has magical equipment and a rolled up piece of carpet that he carries around and levitates on, journeying through the astral plane. He catches me looking at him and smiles - maybe the smile is an invitation to ask for three wishes? I imagine myself opening my wishes jar on the shelf in my hospital room and I write down the first three I pick out at random: to trade places with my sister, to become wealthy but not overly so, and to overcome my eating disorder. Now he is reading something and his lips are miming the words (actually reciting my wishes, bringing them about), so I thank him in my mind.

He gets up to leave, finishes his drink and puts his magic book away in his rucksack. He has done what he needed to do and now he is going to go away and soar through the air on his Aladdin-style carpet of rusty golden swirls. As he exits he accidentally barges into an old woman because he is in a rush to get out of town and on with his day of mystical enchantment, charming young ladies and offering them turns to fly away with him into otherworldly towns full of more marvellous coffee shops.

If I get hit by a bus as I cross the road and die today, I hope Heaven has coffee chains. The genie will go to all the best kinds, ones open at night all night long, overlooking beaches made of an assortment of gemstones. I give him a pet glow-worm to take with him; it talks and lights his genie eyes of

Arabian wonder, living in a cleaned-out pasta jar that he uses instead of candle light. The young ladies either hate his pet worm or love it, finding it whimsical, and they fall in love with him. Then he returns them on his carpet back to the cities where he found them, secretly auditioning them, searching for the right one but he never finds her. Even though he is a magical man he is not looking for a magical lady, not even a beautiful one, but just one that that he doesn't have to rescue; its hard nowadays finding a partner who doesn't need rescuing by another person and a lamp.

I drop my pen there, pick my belongings up and step out into the fresh air. My hands are clumsy and I nearly drop my journal but I make my way back early; I don't quite know why but I want to be back early so I can talk to Carla and Adam and so I can pick a flower for Ron and watch his face light up with mild elation. So I walk back and pick two daffodils. On my return I am immediately greeted by Jess who tells me she is going for a walk around the grounds; she is an insomniac and her dark circles tell of her hard, restless nights.

"Hey, where have you been?" she asks, as vigorous as ever in her manner. I'd say her aura is all the colours of the rainbow because her character is colourful and so is her voice. I associate her with Skittles.

"I just went into town for a coffee. I had to be back for half past eleven, though," I say deceitfully.

"Ah, bet you didn't want to come back to this place, with the weather being nice."

"Yeah, it's a drag in here but never mind," I shrug.

"Who are the daffodils for today?" she says, knowing they are not for her.

"Ron - is he about?" I ask.

"Sure, he's just wandering about somewhere, love."

"Ah, okay. Cheers, Jess," I say. Pacing onto the ward, I press the buzzer. "It's me." They buzz me in and, like I have been away forever, Ron walks towards me hugging me. He is like an eccentric teddy bear. "For you," I say, handing him the daffodils, and he looks delighted like I assumed he would be. I know for sure this is the highlight of his day.

I enter my room, shoving my satchel under my bed, and go to join the others in the television lounge. We are awaiting our dinner, then awaiting the tea trolley, then going for a cigarette in half hourly intervals. I tell all the others, "Man, I can't wait to leave here," and it's a white lie. But they agree with me and we all know that we don't want to leave, because just for a while we are safe to be ourselves. I wish we could all find a genie of our own to grant us three wishes but the truth is that some of the people in here have no wishes. The women wouldn't leave with the genie anyway because magic is something they already have, something they suffer for through their mental illnesses, and adventure is an ongoing thing in their unbalanced minds; so flying around on a magic carpet is not as exciting to them is it sounds. And the staff, well, they don't believe in magic because they have adult minds.

> Golden swirls,
> rolled up worlds,
> late night coffee.
> His name was Johnny
> and he was a genie...

That is the truth. I met a genie in my head and he does own a pet glow-worm called Glowy. But I cannot sleep tonight because I have to figure out how a glow worm glows. So I write a poem and save it in my `phone because I'm too lazy to sit up and write it in my journal.

85

I asked a glow-worm, "Why you do glow?"
because it was something I did not know.
He said, "To make myself pretty."
I replied, "What a pity."
He asked what I meant, so I explained:
"Well, you'd be quite ugly without your light."
He replied, in spite,
"You're one to talk; you're a cruel creature,
your species don't have one likeable feature."
"Fine, I'm out of here, you stupid worm.
You're all for show,
curse you and your silly glow."

The author

Sisters Kimberley and Faye

The memorial

Fieldhead

Author's Dad Paul

Whitby

Beach art

Wakefield

NINE

MY FRIEND MIA AND OTHER CRAZIES

I am riddled with mental illnesses, it appears, including
Bulimia Nervosa.

Yet Mia is very beautiful. We wander together, fingers
entwined, into beauty's painful domain, a world where everybody is thin and beautiful. She is the queen of this land, she and
Ana together. Ana is her sister and is like her but a little more
highly strung, a very controlled persona, whereas Mia is like me;
she lacks self-control and often tells me that she doesn't care if
her oesophagus ruptures because this would be for the best. She
longs for perfection and will never reach it until she dies trying.

In this world, the glossy pages of magazines come to life and
everybody wears clothes that simply hang off their boyish figures.
We sit around drinking coffee and smoking numerous cigarettes, one after the other, anything to suppress our appetites.
Some of us here like the occasional line of charlie because it
keeps us awake and we dance; it is a constant party sometimes.
We like to dance because we can, because we have the confi-
dence to do so. Sometimes though we can't dance and I have
seen girls faint on a regular occasion in this land. They are weak,

but then this only adds to their dainty, fragile looks. Mia is not as skinny as Ana, she is slim but not underweight, and this makes her feel self-conscious.

We all share tips on how to make hunger feel nice. And it does. We sometimes see who can hold out the longest without food. And our worlds become something we are suddenly in control of - that is what we all want, control, because we lack it in the normal world. Mia has many followers, but luckily she is my best friend for now. I would prefer to be acquainted with Ana because she is very influential, but she has a dark side. She is also a glutton for punishment. Anorexia Nervosa and Bulimia Nervosa are sisters and what's funny is that I was like Mia and Kim was like Ana.

Mia cries to me and I cry to her and, like best friends should, we hold one another's hair back as we self-induce vomit after our meals out together. It always feels very disrespectful to the cook, but we just want someone to love us and everybody loves a thin, beautiful girl; we learned this as we grew up, through the media. We then became obsessed with achieving it. And I did achieve this with the help of Prozac and my whole world became something I wanted to be in, purely because I was one of those beautiful girls. That was until Mia came back to me and I copied her inwardly destructive qualities; and due to our binge and purge cycles, which happened several times a day, I became just like her, a normal weight and my lovely bones that once stuck out sharply became covered in a layer of fat. (My weight is up and down - sometimes I am skinny, sometimes fat, and it depends on my mood too.) This is why I currently try to keep Mia at arm's length – I do love her, but she destroys me. And the sometimes beautiful world where she and Ana reside is a place I think I won't visit for a while, although I want to, although I miss it. The painful domain where eating disordered girls and boys live is too far from my reach, because I have made it that way and because I chose to become more than just a girl who is superficial like Mia. She isn't like this because she is a bad person, she's just an emotional anorexic.

I can't deal with her, not while I am trying to get my life together. She has my `phone number but I tell her I don't want to see her every day, like in those seductive times when we used to spend every day together, bingeing and purging, when my mother was out of the house and the cupboards were full. Now she is a friend who remains in the background, I hope. I still induce vomit but I am not under Mia's control anymore. That is final.

Me and Kim used to tell each other all our secrets of how we enjoyed damaging our bodies. We discouraged each other, but we both had addictive personalities and continuous problems with self-image.

I want to be starry,
brighten up the night,
I want to show the heavens
I'll be all dressed in white.

I want to be amazing
in a world that you fear,
getting closer each day,
do you want me here?

I want to be empty
or just enough to let you in,
I just want to show you
and take away your sin.

I want gold to be golden,
silver to stain.
Water washes our souls
but cannot cleanse our pain.

I see trails of diamonds
on a pathway lit by the moon,
but you're about to let me down,
I feel, very soon.

Because I want you to want me;
even if you did I would lie.
My hands are bleeding,
My eyes never cry.

I heard you whisper softly
you wanted to take away my sin;
I can do many things,
but I can never let you in.

Mia helped me to compose this; she can be quite the poet when she is not being affected by the media, when she drops her defences. I've just come across it in a puppy journal that my sister gave me. I was eighteen at the time and attending a Mormon Church; this was just a phase and Kim found it lame, but I attended only for love and the quirky missionary called Liam with his adorable side parting. I loved his American accent. And I loved being told what to do by the church. Kim found this funny; she knew how naïve I was when it came to matters of the heart. To me this was a forbidden love and I craved unrequited love so greatly.

I have just finished baking cookies on the ward. I like to bake and Kim was always great at it. Mel bakes sometimes, his favourite thing being peanut butter cookies; he cuts them with a cookie cutter into love hearts, and I say "Thank you, you're a darling," to him when he hands them to me still warm on a plate. I eat them and then induce vomiting into my bedroom bin. The cleaners did tell me off for this but I don't care too much. And it has been a while since I felt that familiar high that comes after releasing one's emotions into a bin or toilet.

I wish that I wasn't me.
I want to see things
the way you see.

I want you to open up my
eyes so much
and feel the dawn with your touch.

You see emeralds
while I see stone;
write my life for me
so I'm not alone.

I no longer want my views
nor my lies,
my every detail I despise.

Walk with me in the rain,
every drop eases this strain,
and ask me what I want to do...
My only desire is to be like you.

I like to hang on to all the poems I wrote that Kim liked. We both wrote since we were in our teens. Back then I used write love poetry for my first boyfriend - I thought love would become less painful over time but it never did. I also thought my emotions would have matured but they also never did. We loved poetry and gothic clothing, adored dressing in black and wearing Death Kitty labels, sharing our clothes when we were living together. When we weren't I would bring my clothes over in a bag and we would trade items. Social workers used to supervise us when we got together at these times but I didn't mind; it was a free lift and I hated public transport.

Kim spent many years in care and we would text each other our poetry on nights when we couldn't sleep. When we were first separated I cried for days on end, so inconsolable that nobody dared speak to me. Me and Kim texted back and forth and planned our reunion; we planned running away to where nobody would find us. Then we could drink cherry Lambrini and smoke endlessly while applying make-up and pretending we were regular teens, not broken children from a broken home.

Some personality disordered individuals are just by-products of broken homes. Have you ever felt out of place in your own skin? A wallflower, unseen or maybe ignored because you just didn't quite cut it in the ordinary world? If you have and your eccentricities lead to you coming to the conclusion that you must be mentally ill, well, this is like a revelation from some quirky goddess who looks after the mentally ill taking them under her wing. The second you realise that you are 'one of the crazies' is a very satisfying moment, and if you have always struggled to be like 'them' then it is a deeply pleasing moment, a light bulb moment of self-discovery. "I am crazy, these people are crazy, we can all be crazy together." It all feels very endearing, and very new.

On a mental ward you get the feeling of 'family' as we all have to eat together, take morning medication one after the other, and we ask each other "How did you sleep?", which is a pointless question. We use the same showering and bathing areas, then spend the day engaging in small talk with one another and sleep at the same times - if we do sleep, and if not then we hear each other tossing and turning in the room next door through the paper-thin walls. In summery afternoons, we hear how each other's simple tasks went, such as a walk to the Oasis Café on site, or a walk into town to buy toiletries, or the patients who are evidently 'better' tell how their home visits went and how they are petrified of leaving. But like a good friend, each person's words comfort another's anxious mind.

You can see people as they really are, and it's refreshing,
people from all walks of life, just there, just here…
yet not all there and not all here.

Some are indifferent to their own sufferings yet equipped
verbally to help another with their demons, surprisingly better
than the people whose job it is to help us. We talk in deep
sentiments and are provided with a mobile 'phone number
whenever it is needed. Being onboard with the others offers a
new perspective to life and you begin to wonder if you could live
with these people forever. And if you are like me the answer is
"Yes and no". In the beginning it is all very fresh and exciting,
but then comes the impossible task of not quite knowing what to
do or how to act when you are not just generally being 'crazy' or
discussing problems.

People love eccentric people, and they love crazy people
and crazy people's stories, for they are always very 'out there' and
normal people (unaffected with craziness) more often than not
hold themselves back in thought, opinion and action. These
kinds of people are weak characters.

Crazy people seem to lack either the ability to keep their
thoughts and opinions internalised, or they have been crazy for
so long that they don't realise that some things are better kept
secret than exposed to reality and judgement. Maybe actually
they just do not care, because they realise that life shouldn't be
taken seriously and that this is a fact that must be learned fast.
Crazy people can interact with each other in a very relaxed and
honest manner; sometimes no thoughts are held back during
conversations, so conversations are usually very colourful. This is
why I chose only to maintain friendships with strictly crazy
people, keeping the normal bores at bay.

Crazies, to me, are people who have been stripped down
and are now very raw and real, the reality totally ironic. Some
people are afraid of this kind of rawness, and sanity is sometimes

a defence mechanism in a sense because when one drops their sanity they become like children, exposed to painful emotions and desires. Yet when this stage is reached, all one has to do is remember to breathe. This is when the spirit is freed. And then insanity as also used as a defence mechanism, very subtly, as a way to offer 'explanations' to others for unacceptable (though not necessarily morally wrong) behaviour.

The flip side to the benefits of craziness is the simple fact that routine becomes boring fast, the sweet nothings of mental illness grow tedious and a regular environment makes you wander, for we all yearn for change when things have remained the same over a period of time. For me it is shorter than other people's time limits. Although it can be comfortable staying in the same state, being the same person day after day, it grows heavily boring and boredom is intolerable; it forces you into a contemplative state and this is the stage I have now more or less reached. I am now contemplating whether being crazy is something I like or dislike, and whether if I dislike it, that the reason is because I am used to it. So maybe a better idea is for people to go crazy *sometimes*, let go sometimes and at other times keep it together, so that the crazy times are more pleasurable and not taken for granted.

Hanging out with other mentally ill people loses its novelty fast and one slowly becomes accustomed to their own craziness; it is then very hard to know what to do with yourself when you are not being crazy. When you are not having a breakdown, when you are not on a mental ward but are in recovery and in the normal world, what do you do? Who are you? How do you act around people? I was, or am, a crazy girl and nothing more, but can that be enough to get people to like you, to distinguish you? Well, no, because that is only a part of you and craziness is not an art in itself, only when it is directed into something. It can smother you if you let it, and not allow you to have any other characteristics. But if you keep it at a close yet safe distance, it can breathe life into many artsy areas of life, adding colours that seem more vibrant if painted with the hands of a crazy man, or craziness can twist and turn throughout a fantastic novel. I try to direct my overwhelming emotions into creativity, creating with the overspill of craziness and emotions.

But what will the other patients, my friends, do? And will the ties that bind us together break when we all start to lead as close to ordinary lives as we can? Maybe. I mean, some of us will get better, others not, and we will become mismatched in our levels of craziness and go our separate ways. This can be kind of sad, because some of us found ourselves during our stay on the mental wards, we found kindred spirits and felt we had a 'family' - although we didn't voice it. We became more than the misfits of society, rather 'the thinkers' who blend together either sitting in silence as the staff patrol, or mindlessly chattering about topics ranging from everyday things to the nature of reality. In these ways we play the part of happy people together, and we act it out so well that we find ourselves feeling happy, as we attend to the activities the ward offers, such as arts and crafts, cooking, meditation or karaoke on Friday take-away nights.

Getting to the stage where it is evident you actually qualify as being mentally ill is something you don't see yourself coming to until you get there. It feels like an accident. You have accidentally broken down all the boundaries you once had and fully succumb to all life's greatest things. Perhaps it all started for you from a simple, single inquisitive thought that led to a deep depression, or maybe you were sitting watching the sunset and you began a trail of thought that wouldn't go away, and that's when your common sense and sanity dissolved. Your mind has unravelled, the rational thoughts gone, making way for a new mind that is now more alert, more in tune with the Earth but also unfortunately broken by the magnitude of your thoughts and realisations. And then it's hard to live a normal life so you don't, you throw yourself into madness either into a looney bin or some other service. This has its benefits:

- eating and sleeping when your body needs and wants it, napping as you please, and scoffing biscuits rather than sticking to meals;

- no work or needless hours slaving away just to get by, and time to learn about who you are;

- no bills (only adults pay bills);

- every interaction you make with the outside world on your own terms, because suddenly your friends and family are the ones who are asking when *you* want to see them and what *you* want to do;

- a feeling of what it is like to live in Wonderland without actually physically going there;

- befriending the greatest people you will ever meet in your life and realising that they definitely beat your previous friends.

These benefits are tempting and of course if you are unwell you must take them and embrace them. I find it is very hard now to stop myself trying to manipulate my way in; it takes willpower to resist having a breakdown every other week just to get purposely put onto a mental ward. This may seem crazy, but it is what some crazies do.

At the moment I am far too accustomed to craziness to enjoy it - but you might. My starry imagination is boring me, falling in love is losing its highs, and taking morning psychotropic medications is becoming a chore. I cannot glamorise mental illness anymore because I have lived in it a while now. I realise it is not as much fun as I first imagined when I stepped onto Fieldhead Priory 2, my heart ablaze with wasted passion that needed a release.

I apologise for fast-forwarding you into my feelings after I left the ward, but being borderline means constant change.

TEN

CELESTIAL BEINGS

Carl is grinning like a moron. He loves any chance he gets to talk to another about 'his crew' and I love his schizophrenic story-telling immensely. (He has amphetamine-induced psychosis.) I cross my legs, sitting on the floor of the women's lounge, and he sits opposite me like a man-child. It is weird to see a fully grown man sit there, drawing a picture on a lined notebook of a Clever Monster. He tears off the page, handing it to me; he has drawn an equilateral triangle with an eye in the centre of it.

"This is Clever Monster," he says.

"Tell me more," I plead and his words roll out in excitement. As he speaks his voice changes into one of a giddy youngster.

"He's a clever monster and he always wanted to be a monster. He's on the crew, a mathematical genius. I saved him from Hell, you see, I dragged him out and kitted him up and now he's one of the crew. He's a fucking genius. He goes in and out of x-y-z dimensions."

"That's amazing, Carl," I say as daylight fades and the yellow curtains make me cringe. I don't like yellow. Well, anything yellow apart from the sun, daffodils and sunflowers. Me and Adam went picking daffodils yesterday morning in the grounds.

101

"It is, ain't it?" he says. "I am U, the one true god - the messiah," he says, stressing the importance of this. "One true god." His voice is becoming louder as he continues, "'Evil' is 'live' spelled backwards, e-v-i-l," his voice booms as he says each letter with conviction.

I don't know what this has to do with anything so I ask, "Is Clever Monster evil?" Carl seems offended so he takes a deep breath and sits up in a good posture; he starts again from the beginning, attempting to tell it to me as straight and coherently as possible. I can see this is a strain for him.

"I pulled Clever Monster out of Hell. Before he was a monster he was a laugh, an absolute laugh, but he always wanted to be a monster though so I made him into one. He stays in x-y-z dimensions as much as possible and you can't see it but I can, because you're not tuned into the right frequencies and you walk with a bar in front of your eyes..." He presses his index finger to the bridge of his nose. "Everybody has an eye here. It lights up, but most people don't know."

"Ah, that's weird," I say.

"I know it is. I can open your mind if you want."

I have the Pretty Reckless playing in the background so I filter out the music to put my full attention on Carl's words in case he asks me to recite anything he's said at a later date. "Oh how do you do that?" I ask innocently.

"I'll show you. Lie down on your back," he says, pulling a gammy half-smoked roll-up from his pocket and sparking it up. I don't know what else to do so I lie flat on my back. He bends down and blows smoke from his roll-up into my nostrils. I notice Liz, another patient, looking through the window as she walks past to get to the smokers' cage. I lie very still.

"Right, stand up," he says, grabbing my hand and pulling me easily to my feet. He is strong. "Look into my eyes." He pushes his forehead against mine and our eyes are about a centimetre or two apart; his eyes shake while I just stand with my hands by my sides. He holds the stare for around five seconds. "Stay still," he says, then shouts something I don't quite catch into my ear. Ouch! His voice goes right through me. I stand bewildered and he is stood in front of me as if he wants me to say something so I do.

"I felt that."

"Good, you can see the world now and not just watch it go by," he says.

Because I don't know what else to say, I decide that I need a cigarette due to the mind-blowing experience I am supposed to have had. I feel a dummy because Liz saw me; most patients entertain Carl's ramblings but most wouldn't just lie there as he blew smoke up their nostrils. I run out of the room and catch Liz in the corridor.

"I don't have a clue what just happened to me. Carl just blew smoke up my nostrils," I say.

We both giggle together. I had a conversation with Liz yesterday; she is nice, with blonde hair in tight curls, a nice strawberry blonde. Yesterday evening as she was sprawled out (she is overweight) on the women's lounge sofa watching soaps, I walked in and we had a little heart to heart. We both share loss. She told me she had found her husband dead. He had slipped in the shower and, I presume, smashed his skull and bled to death; this was five years ago, and she told me he loved rugby and played on Eastmoor, which I told her is the estate my mother lives in.

I offer Liz for a cig - more of an offer for some chit chat - and she accepts, so we stand together in the smoking cage and she tells me how her house is being decorated and she doesn't want to go home and be alone. Carl then steps outside and takes a seat next to Liz. They both sit there and compassion is the mood. Carl is staring ahead of him, like he does, muttering something about Venus and Mars, whom he knows on a personal level. He says they are married. Me and Liz are rudely talking over him and he looks lonely, then he turns to me.

"I am loveless, you know," and at this instant I realise that hearing voices doesn't make someone any less lonely, which was a theory I had when I first encountered him.

"I don't think you are," I say.

"Yeah, you are a lovely guy, Carl," Liz says sympathetically. He doesn't consciously want sympathy though and the soreness of his revelation does not disappear, going by the look on his face.

"No, I am not bothered that I am loveless, it's not worth it anyway. I can't be loved because I am U, the one true god, and females can't handle it. My ex left me for another man and since then I can't be loved," he says.

"I won't find love again," Liz says, though she is warm-hearted, with such a friendly face. "Since my husband died I don't want to fall in love."

"Did he die?" Carl asks.

"Yeah, he's been gone for years now," Liz says. And realising we are all different, our individual pains from loss have us somewhat invisibly and tenderly connected, even if it's just for this instant, and we make the most of this moment.

"I lost my sister," I offer.

"I have felt loss to such a magnitude that I can't love," Carl says sincerely.

"I think I am loveless too," I sigh.

"Same here," Liz says.

Carl tells us all about how he came from normality to the looney bin. He describes a slow decline and life's inevitable triggers. He says he went to kill his ex-girlfriend's lover, but changed his mind. I think Clever Monster told him not to do it. Clever Monster distracted him with equations and algebra. We ask Carl if he's in touch with 'the other side' and Liz fiddles with her wedding ring as she turns to him with watery blue eyes.

"Is my husband in Heaven?" she asks.

"Yes he is, but boys don't live again and girls do, girls are reborn. So, aye, he might in Heaven," Carl says.

"Is my sister in Heaven"? I ask.

"Aye, she might be but she's probably been reborn - she may be a baby," he replies.

"Will I join my husband when I die, Carl?" Liz is making her finger go a little red from fiddling with her ring that ties her to her deceased loved one. I have nothing to tie me; I don't even own a single photograph of my loved one.

"Maybe, if you're not reborn." He nearly spirals into a speech but I interrupt him.

"Can't you make Liz into an angel, then she can be with her husband?"

"I could make you into a celestial being, yeah?" Carl looks at Liz who nods.

"If you would," she says. "I miss my husband, Carl."

Carl looks at me. "You're going to be the earth element, though, Elisa? Or a goddess?"

"Well, that suits me," I say, smiling, and actually believing that Carl can make this happen. I look at Liz and she looks back at me, believing it too. We are the only three out at the minute, then Beth opens the door.

"Elisa, Liz and Carl," she says as she ticks us off on the clip-board nurses carry for hourly checks. "Supper time soon."

Liz is dead now, as I am writing; she committed suicide and, after thirty-odd admissions into Fieldhead due to her attempts, she was at last successful and got to become a celestial being. Her death was a shame, but if she is with her husband then she is at peace. She was approximately thirty years old.

I get up as Liz and Carl are ready for tea and toast, but I go to take a bath and light up a cig there, which is risky as the staff are like hounds. I let the Radox bath salts relax me and fall into a state of contemplation; I have my `phone on the side of the bath because as I finish my cig and dock it out I immerse myself under the water, hold my breath, and I can hear the music amplified under the water, Enya's Exile echoing into my ears. I hold my breath and imagine myself as a goddess with exquisite looks and Liz as a celestial being, then break through the water and take a deep breath of air, leaning my head back against the tub. I feel like me. But I don't know what me is.

> The clever monster was oh so clever,
> he spoke through digits and riddles.
> He was a monster, he lived forever
> until he was ended with anti-psychotic pills.

I sit in my room and pull a bottle of whiskey out of from under my bed. I take a swig and it burns my throat. Mel left it here last night. After I had chatted to Carl and Liz, I came into my room because I missed the time I spend alone with Mel. I needed that swig as I have just seen the doctor and discussed some deep issues with him.

Merion and Peter, the Family Liaison Officers, joined in on my ward round and told me that Otak had pleaded guilty. At first, see, he tried to put some blame on me. Let me tell you, if I was going to have some involvement in anybody's death, it would not have been anyone other than Otak. They told me that I did not have to stand in the witness box and any evidence could be done through a video link. Then they said I would have a while to wait until the trial because the date had been moved on an extra few months. So I am now allowed out for as long as I want, as long as I am back for 9 p.m. And this scares me because I do not want to tread into the outside world. This put the fear of God into me so I start writing...

106

The most beautiful sounding word in the English language is not 'cellar-door' it is 'melancholy' and the second is 'Tobias'. The third is debatable. This is my thought for the day. 'Kimberley' is an invalid word to the world now; otherwise I would of course tell you that this is the single most beautiful word.

I decide that I should perhaps spend my afternoon in the sun, so I go to sit outside in a part of the hospital just past the car park that holds a magical patch planted with flowers and vegetables. There are Chinese lanterns hanging here also, which I really like, and I often wonder if I could shrink inside one and fly away. Or become a pixie, perhaps? I was told that the patch is magical by Carla, who goes there to smoke her weed. I invite Liz to come and sit with me and she agrees as it would be a shame to sit indoors in this weather. The courtyard on the ward doesn't quite cut it and it has a huge painting on the wall opposite the window that the staff earwig out of. On the courtyard red-brick wall is what looks like a painting produced by a toddler of a huge spider and big flowers with four or five petals and a smiley face. We sit and talk about how we will become celestial beings one day. She accuses me of being in love with Tobias and I reject this idea initially but as I blush I realise that I am giving it away. So I come clean.

"Okay, I like him quite a lot," I say, lifting my hands in mock surrender.

"I knew it. Well, you're still young so don't let that bastard ex of yours ruin your future relationships," she says.

"Don't you think it's a little too soon for me to even think about a guy in that way?" I ask.

"Not at all. Don't wait around for things in life because life won't wait around for you," she says, inhaling her menthol cig. I see a shadow of a man walking towards this area and I am startled as I recognise it as Tobias. Liz jumps to her feet when she sees him too, and nudges me. "Better leave you to it."

"Okay, see ya later, Liz," I reply. My throat closes, so I pull out a cigarette; it might open my lungs to new possibilities as he grows closer. Just above the road line is a wave of midday heat. I stand up and Iscuttle around to find an appropriate position to sit in, then take to the bench and wonder if potatoes are growing in the ground - just a random thought. Tobias looks like he is in need of a blood fix... I shuffle over on the bench and he sits next to me and I feel happy to know he is not completely bedridden now. He smells of B.O. As I turn my head to look at him, he is staring directly in front of him and I wonder if I'm invisible, so I speak as softly and as clearly as I can.

"Hey, nice day isn't it?" I say and he responds with a grunt so I continue, "So... did you get my second note?"

"Yes, I did and I can't read," he says bluntly.

"Sorry, I didn't realise. It wasn't important anyway," I reply. I had suspected dyslexia but hoped the note would just make him curious and prompt him to speak more to me. He pulls a bottle of Jack Daniels from his inside coat pocket. His coat is a black parka which is not well matched to the sweltering weather conditions. He takes a swig. Well, I guess it could be stressful being a vampire and all.

"Can I have a drink?" I ask, as I've left my bottle inside.

"You shouldn't drink on medication," he replies, looking at me at last.

"Oh, well, I haven't taken medication today," I say and he hands me the bottle. I take a swig and it burns my throat nicely, so maybe now I can get my words out less clumsily. "Want a cig?" I ask, feeling the amorous sun on my shoulders.

"Yes, please." He takes one and I stare at his hands which look so fair and smooth. They're Mel's hands.

"Do you want me to play some music?" I offer my `phone out.

"Yes, can I have a look through?" he asks so I hand him the `phone. He slides his finger over the touch screen and comes to a playlist I have of The Smiths and I feel thankful that he likes Morrissey too as he is my hero and I love his outrageous statements on animal rights and so on. "So what did your note say?" he asks. I am jittery inside but outwardly I maintain my cool and collected image.

"Just that we should meet up on the astral plane," I say and he smiles - I cannot gauge what kind of smile this is so I probe further. "Do you think that could be a possibility?" He bursts into laughter and now I feel like a small, inexperienced teenager. "Bad joke," I say biting my lip, but he looks at me and his face turns from laughter to disappointment.

"No, no, I would love to," he says honestly.

"Okay, well… tonight maybe?" I ask timidly.

"Yeah, sure thing."

His voice is gruff and lacks enthusiasm but his eyes say otherwise. We sit then in silence and I can't break it and I don't want to; he places his hand on top of mine and there is a space between us on the bench which we both keep. We sit for another half an hour and listen intently to Morrissey's voice as we pass the liquor back and forth between one another. I love how rare he is to come across; he is like a rare bird in my eyes and I guess I am just a common one, but maybe in another lifetime we will be like two doves and we'll eat vermillion berries from the gardens on Fieldhead together. I get up when he lifts his hand from mine and tells me, "I have enjoyed spending time with you."

"Me too. Well, see you around," I beam as I leave him. I feel giddy towards night-time; it's becoming the only environment I can see clearly in.

Confined in an imprisonment
of heart-shaped corridors,
that are my mind's paradise.
They are not complete illusions.
I suffer from delusions
and he is in it with me -
seeing this state of madness,
wandering corridors of cream,
I see his face, it's like a dream.
But it's not a dream,
it's heavenly candyfloss ice-cream.
Love in the asylum.

(I wrote this in the medication queue.
We have to wait half an hour before they dish the meds out.)

The following day I decide I should get my feelings out of the way, so I walk round to the Fieldhead garden and sit down on the bench, then text Carl to get him to ask Tobias to come and meet me. So he does and Tobias arrives shortly afterwards. I ask myself whether this man owns any more than one outfit. But he has his dark brown hair in a side parting and I find this dashing, very comely.

"So, how's it going?" he says, taking a seat next to me.

"Fine," I say. Then I cannot think of where to start, so I ask him outright, knowing that he is not the kind of guy to pick up on hints. "Have you ever been in love?"

He answers sharply, "No."

"What, like never?" I say. This is foreign to me as I fall in love every week with a new potential suitor. To me, infatuation equals true love.

"No, never." He looks a little bashful.

"Would you ever like to fall in love?" I ask.

"Why not?" he replies.

"With me?" I immediately regret my words.

"I don't know you," he responds quietly.

"Getting to know someone is part of the process in which you fall in love," I say, feeling stupid and kicking myself for saying such a thing. I begin fiddling nervously and take from my bag my back-up bottle of Jack Daniels that I bought this morning just for this moment, in case I needed liquor courage.

"I guess so," he responds and looks at me at last. How I wish he gave more than the briefest answers. I take a swig.

"Can I have a drink?" he asks.

"Of course," I say, handing him the bottle. "Don't worry, I don't love you."

"Alright," he says.

And this is when it hits me that he is too unwell to love at the minute, and maybe he can't love? Maybe he's one who loves but only at a distance, kind of like me? Maybe none of this will matter when I leave here and never think of him again, never think of the days I couldn't eat or sleep because he had sent me high, never think of all the notes I wrote to him? More than likely he will become one of those people whom I may see around from time to time, and I will smile and say "Hi" but he will not recognise me.

In my head, I fantasise that we are just starting out on an epic romance - only in a fantasy world though, as I cannot trust him enough to start anything worth starting in person anyway. I live on fantasies. I hope that one day Tobias does fall in love and whoever he falls in love with loves him back. I hope his head clears up. But the Tobias I met on Priory 2 is going to be held in my head and stored away as a mystery, one who loved me then left me high and dry, the strange vampire who could not let his petals unfurl and feed me the nectar I craved. This is okay. It's alright. Real life romance is overrated.

"I'm leaving here when I find somewhere to live," I continue.

"Hope it goes well for you. I think I'll always be in here," he says.

"No, one day you will get out and you will get well," I reply.

"I don't want to get out or get well," he says seriously. And then it hits me that, for the minority of people, this is a way of life and not something to be recovered from.

"Well, I just want you to know one thing..." I take a deep breath and smile as I speak, "I think you are amazing."

"Thanks," he says.

And just like that I get up and leave him to his own company, which is clearly how he wants to live his life and is not a bad thing. As long as he is not lonely, it is not a bad thing. Solitude is nice when loneliness is absent. I go back onto the ward and begin sketching how I see Tobias, stood there in the cage with a cigarette hanging from his mouth. Never could an image be more breathtaking and as I draw I become neutral in my feelings for him. I like this neutrality.

Cigarettes, baby,
do you want a drag?
Breathe me in,
inhale my sadness,
spark up my mind
with no intentions.
Please would you
take my lungs to new dimensions?

Watch me in the cage,
trying to catch the night.
Cigarettes, baby,
can you read or write?
I wrote you a letter,
my adoration, black and white.
Cigarettes, baby,
can I have a light?

ELEVEN

RANDOM MAN

I take a seat in the conservatory joined onto the Oasis Café and overlooking the Criminal Ward for the mentally ill. I get comfortable in my position and flick through a very boring homes magazine, eating a Club bar. There is nobody else here other than me and some students who usually work in the Psychology block, an outpatient service. They are obviously on a break.

A random man, who must have quietly been in the pool room at the back end of the conservatory, steps out like a tall, lanky giant, around six feet two. He has a huge grin and immediately paces over to me, past the students who look at him as though he is a different species; he is the kind of patient whom you can tell is a patient upon first sight. I look over to my right to see if he has mistaken me for somebody else, then quickly look back at him. He is looking at me as if I am some long lost daughter of his.

"I know you, you're the girl I met at Alton Towers," he says.

"I think you have the wrong person," I smile politely.

"No, I haven't. It's me - don't you remember me? We fell in love," he says and his smile almost reaches his eyes. "Jody, it's me. We fell in love, you and me did, with our blue eyes, that day at Alton Towers."

"I've never been to Alton Towers," I say subtly, emphasising that there is no way on Earth I could have met this man before. Ever. I have, however, seen him on the ward. As he stands there before me with a pool cue in his bony hand, I remember him now - he's the candle man. "I think we said 'hello' to each other on Priory," I say, offering an explanation.

"You're Jody, aren't you? Come on, Jody, you remember me? I had my leather jacket on and you had your little denim shorts on and a pink tie-die tee-shirt, so cute ya looked. Your hair was a mess from the rides. I haven't aged since then either - look into my eyes, I have blue eyes like you, angel eyes." His eyes are a piercing blue, but that is his only nice physical feature.

The students are pretending they haven't finished their coffee so they can be nosey. In my opinion, this is slightly irritating because students who are studying Psychology or mental health subjects constantly seem to apply to all regular scenarios what they have read in a textbook or heard in one of their lectures. If idiocy were a mental illness, they would be the textbook cases. You know the kind of student I am talking about – those who have never so much as lost a set of keys in their life, or had to stay in a bed that is not their own with their own fluffed-up pillows of comfort and ambition. Now, I am not one of those people who have become bitter towards more privileged people because of my own hardships; I can tell the difference between an idiot and a bright spark, though, regardless of how privileged or hardshipped someone is. It just so happens that the privileged classes have a higher rate of ignorance than the lower classes, and ignorance can turn into downright idiocy. Of course, in the lower classes there are a lot of idiots about too, and an uneducated idiot is worse than an educated one. Academia gives some idiots a golden degree, a means to reference things they don't understand at all. After they leave education they can present themselves as doctors, mental health nurses and psychologists and so on, and pretend they care.

"I can't believe you don't remember me," the man says. His dark hair looks rather greasy, slightly greying too. He sits on the chair opposite me, putting his elbows up on the small round table.

"You know, you might just have to refresh my memory," I say, hoping that the students will become disappointed when they think I actually do remember him and they can't apply 'suffers delusions' to him.

"Yeah, okay, I'll tell you how we met. This should be a nice little trip down Memory Lane and its windy, narrow roads. Jody, you are silly, aren't ya?" He squints as he looks at me, sat there in my black lace skirt and stripy socks. I guess I do look rather gothic today. Mel did dress me, though.

Two young students pick up their finished cups, walk past me and smile, not a nice smile but false. I smile back equally falsely, noticing their nails are kind of too long and plastic, French manicured. Maybe I am being too judgemental. Let's face it, I am in no position to judge, but their smiley faces and formal name tags are annoyingly superficial. Then I sit still and mindful, pretending I am Jody whilst the man 'refreshes my very poor memory'. He leans forward eager to start; he has coffee breath and it is making me want to vomit, but I hide this.

"Well, it was the summer of 2001 so we are going more than ten years back now. I had taken time out of work - I worked as a carpenter back then. Anyhow, me and a bunch of friends, you know, the lads from the local pub, well, we decided we would all go to Alton Towers. You know, do something different, something that would give us a bit of a laugh. I was just as handsome then as I am now."

As you are now?

"I drove a van at the time so we drove over, about six of us. We all got stoned on the way and the drive in itself was fun enough, see, it wasn't very often any of us left Wakefield, not off our own backs anyway 'cause a couple of my friends were married. I'd never really found a lass I could fall in love with - falling in love always felt like a challenge for me. So we reached Alton Towers. I remember it like yesterday. We jumped out of the van. I looked like John Travolta, stood there with my leather jacket on and my comb in my pocket."

As he says this, I notice a fine-toothed comb poking out of his light denim jacket pocket. My first ever self-harm happened with a fine-toothed comb when I was around twelve years old.

"Anyway, we went on all the big rides. The first one we went on was the Corkscrew, which had a couple of old ladies on who became quite scared when the ride got stuck for five minutes. Me and the lads found this funny. Mostly, though, the old ladies stuck to the teacups and smaller shit like that..."

His voice trails off and I begin to fall into a daydream, or should I say a day nightmare as I remember sitting with Otak in the flat of horrors and texting my sister: "What do you think of Otak? Do you think I've made the right decision moving in with him?" Otak had only just started his controlling behaviour at this point and had just finished giving me a telling off for talking to the guys who work at the smoothie bar in town.

"Well, I guess so, but I thought you didn't like him?" she replied. She was right – I'd met him in care and then after I left care I scribbled his face out of photographs and told myself he was as good as dead. See, he was annoyingly pervy in how he spoke to me while I was in care. He often asked for kisses, and I often swore at him and told him to drop dead.

"I didn't, but I didn't want to stay in that hostel. He's alright as a friend," I replied to Kim.

"Yeah, I guess so, but he thinks you're together," she responded.

This was true and I hadn't thought about it much when I first moved in on impulse with all my bags. I had been spending the weeks leading up to the crucial decision hanging around with him. He'd been bringing my food shopping over and helping me out financially with bus fares to get over to Wakefield to see my Mum or Dad. He'd met Sammy too, on my eighteenth birthday – I'd been kicked out a month before.

"Jody, are you listening?" the candle man says.

My expression is vacant. I can see it reflected in the glass of the conservatory as I hit reality hard, so I snap out of it and say, "Yes, of course."

"No, you're not." But he continues anyway and I reminisce again.

I was sitting with Kim and Otak and we were all drinking. I had tried to leave him earlier on in the day. I'd gone to Kim's new flat in Wakefield and we'd sat down doing some artwork and she had told me that I needed to leave him when I confessed to her that he'd been threatening me with knives. I told her everything, how a few nights before he had raped me with a huge kitchen knife by his side, anally raped me after returning home from work.

I see other images now, the flashing kind. He has a sewing needle in his hand.

"Stay quiet," he says.

Then I am undressing. We are in the shower now. I am cold and he is biting me. I stand there. I am going to die. I am going to die tonight. Wait, no I'm not.

"Jody, you're not listening," he says, standing up. I let him walk away with a pool cue in his hands. I look across to the table next to me and a woman is eating a Snickers bar. My heart rate becomes triggered into a state of hard, fast beats, my palms sweat as another flash hits me...

We are in the car, Sammy's car. Sammy is dead. We stop at a petrol station. The yellow sign stings my eyes. My legs are bound with cable. He walks back towards the car with two Snickers bars in his hand and offers me one.

Then I am running, running away from him in the middle of Dover. I jump over someone's garden fence.

"Phone the fucking police!" I shout.

Then I snap out of it and watch the candle man standing at the entrance to Priory 2. He waves to me. I smile and get up to leave the café.

TWELVE

CONNECTING TO NATURE

PTSD, oh, set me free
into society
where I intimate a rose.
Can they see?
I am dying, dying,
this is the nature of PTSD.

Can you dissect my half-heart? It is summer but my half-heart is stuck in December and its ever-so-short daylight hours. I have the trial coming up very shortly and I cannot take this reality. But I will face it, not because I am strong - I just appear hard as nails because I have to. And the sun won't let me simply die. I have a vitamin deficiency so I step outside into the courtyard where I spent yesterday, allowing the sun to absorb my pain. Now I am back for another session and as I stare at the sky I notice that there is after all such a thing as 'sky blue'; I mistook it as a drab grey-blue in my past.

A patient is sitting on the opposite bench, rocking back and forth and blurting out explicit language in a way she cannot control. My Dad came to see me last night and he promised to come again this evening. He cheered a lot of the patients up yesterday as he told us facts about space, while the staff made it known by their facial expressions that they were not pleased by his presence. It was nice to see him and share common beliefs, beliefs that we have a future, the potential to speak to the world and the drive to achieve this. We are going to tell the world what we have held in for so long. I want to tell the world that I am in love with my past, that I am just a girl, an ordinary girl, and I haven't let PTSD take me. I want to tell the world to smile with me.

The courtyard has whitebells planted in soil that is well nourished. I wish my heart was nourished, a heart nourished with love and care, the kind of care that is unconditional. I find this kind of care hard to believe in when I think of it in any other context than that of my sister. I like whitebells; they are similar to bluebells but white represents purity. When me and my sister were younger, we watched my mother watering bluebells; she suggested talking to them so they would grow faster, so me and my sister did as we sucked ice lollies that dripped down our sticky hands.

I made a friend yesterday with one of the plants and it told me that I should spend more time in nature, to keep my soul as healthy as possible, so now I am doing just that. I lie on the central bench, my `phone on the table, my face turned to the side because I cannot find my shades. I am watching patients walk by on the corridors, and the courtyard door is open as I left it. Adam is seated in the main lounge; today he was excellent at making me laugh with jokes I could actually comprehend. He is good like that - a few months ago I thought nobody could ever make me laugh how Kim did.

I watch Tobias walk by and he looks at me with a smouldering intensity. We don't speak to each other, we have come to unspoken agreement that we should avoid each other. This is how damaged people work; that is to say, damaged people struggle with the right words to vocalise. This is okay with me, in fact it is ideal. I must focus on the trial that is to take place soon. I must focus on getting my social life back and I must do so without holding everybody else's personalities up against the flawless one that Kim possessed. She will always be up on that pedestal, though. She always was, always will be.

So I begin to talk to the daffodils because this is the way forward. I then text all of my friends whom I have avoided for a good few months. The time before the last time I spent with Natalie (the time before Clarence) was when she came to stay at my aunt's and uncle's. We were both very drunk as we had been out to the pub and we'd decided that we wanted to go to the grave. It was midnight but this didn't matter - we needed to go there and then. So my uncle drove us up there. We all sat down. We got out a butterfly candle to light for her, one that we'd bought from a garden centre a few weeks before with the intention of lighting it every night for her. I sat right on top of the grave and it was still raised from the newly planted soil, which apparently sinks after time. I sat and looked at the wooden cross – there wasn't a headstone yet - but I didn't sit for long before I began flailing around and desperately digging up the soil with my bare hands, at which point my uncle picked me up over his shoulder and took me back home.

Now I text Natalie and ask her to meet me for a coffee in town, then I text my Mum and tell her I want to see Faye. She agrees and says she will bring Faye up to the hospital. There is a visiting room that is suited to kids and has play things in it. So she does, and Faye sits colouring in a picture of a house, and I see the sadness in both my Mum's and Faye's eyes as I make small talk. Our eyes are probably reflecting each other's pain and I imagine I have this same subtle sadness within my own. This is a sadness that will always be in our eyes, even when we are smiling, which we are now as we joke about recent events such as how a shopkeeper behaved the other day towards my Mum in Marks and Spencer. My Mum used to get me and Kim clothes from Marks and Spencer, often matching items too.

My Mum leaves and I give Faye a big hug and realise that, just as I thought my family had forgotten me, I had forgotten them. We had forgotten that we all still have a reason to live, for each other, we who are left in the aftermath of a double homicide, we who now have broken chests and grieving hearts.

I stroll through a poppy field behind Fieldhead, just down the lane, after my mother and Faye have left to go home and make their tea at a table with two chairs. There will be three for holidays and festivities. But never four again. I take my `phone out and begin taking pictures, then sit in the middle of the poppy field and imagine the poppies are bleeding out onto the untouched soil. And they speak to me, they can feel my pain. The truth is that everything is connected and Mother Nature mourns for Sammy and Kim as much as we do. When I say 'we' I also mean all who suffer from grief; we may feel alone in our suffering but we are not alone for that would mean that our suffering didn't extend beyond ourselves and it does.

I lie down and laugh a little, because the clouds are making funny shapes and I am in a looney bin. I look over into the distance past the trees and wish that people did not smoke outside the hospital doors. Then I listen to the wind. I do not expect straightforward answers for the questions I have, and I am aware that some things go unanswered. They will go round in circles and will never reach an answer because there is no end to a circle. I do not question this any further but take out a cigarette instead and vow to Mother Nature that I will continue to live in an attempt to provide the world with something. My writing? My story? A lesson perhaps? At least, I shall make people smile whenever I can. Kim approves of this.

I take to my feet, close my eyes and run through the field, each footstep pounding hard on the ground. I feel invigorated and for a split second I don't mind being me and this scares me so I scream. All at once I feel as if my lungs are going to cave in, for I am going to make it, I am going to leave this place after they find me somewhere to live. I am going to see Otak go down and then I am going to make Kim proud. It is as simple as that.

Me and you,
wishing to form galaxies,
star drivers, we were.
Through the constellation Pleiades,
we were complete crazies,
you and me.

On Mars,
longing for the expansion of stars,
stuck, speechless,
we are reckless.
In the Dark Age,
stuck in a book, the wrong page,
me and you.

Let us gaze
through the telescope
into our distant past.
We don't have a clue
about anything but me and you.

Ultraviolent light
your star-struck eyes emit.
But to grief I cannot commit.

Ron is crying because the sunset is fading as black clouds take over and Ron has lost his magic. So now I am helping him find it.

"You may have misplaced it?" I suggest.

"No, I haven't misplaced it, magic comes from within," he says.

"Well, then you have to find it within yourself," I reply.

"How?" he says, and this shocks me a little as he never usually asks questions. Usually he's all answers.

"Maybe you just need to do something that inspires your magic to come out?" I say, feeling like a spiritual agony aunt.

"There is nobody else to heal. I have healed everyone. My magic surfaces when I am healing someone and then stays on the surface a couple of days after," he replies, running his hands through his dark curly hair, looking frustrated.

"What else do you like doing when you're not healing people or talking to dead people?"

Twilight is such a special hour. The black clouds that are covering the sunset are but gifts to the sky, for the sky in twilight becomes a dome under which we all slow down in our daily activities and maybe, if we are bright, we take time to appreciate our lives. Now he frowns as though discomfited by his inability to answer my question.

"Hmm, I read," he says, "and I used to do art work."

"Bingo!" I clasp my hands together joyously. "That's what you need to do to get your magic back, then." I still do not know exactly what it means to have lost your magic, so Ron tells me; he only knows he has lost it because he feels low in mood. I am still not getting what he says but I understand magic to be in the act of creation, the creation of something beautiful. Think of the fact that we are all made from stardust, which has a magical feeling to it; we are all creations and we are beautiful (apart from the world's monsters - they were not intentional creations).

Think of the awe-inspiring statue of David, or a song that you cannot get enough of, the kind that takes you into different realms inside your head - is that not also magic? A nurse pops her head round the door. "Don't leave your tab ends on the floor, guys. I swept up not long ago and look at the floor already." We ignore her and the grey floor of the cage, cigarette butts gathered at its edges.

"You may be onto something there," he says, and his frustrated expression lifts. As I watch this, I feel like I may be magic myself and maybe my words hold some hidden magic in them. That would be cool. He winks at me and leaves instantly.

I spend a few hours reading with Mel and he points something out to me. "This is the first time you have sat and read something for a while and actually let yourself be drawn into it."

"I know," I say. We are in my study (aka my hospital bedroom) and I have just eaten supper for the first time in ages.

"You are getting yourself back."

"What do you mean?" I ask, missing the end of the sentence I was reading in my new read, We Need To Talk About Kevin.

"Well, you know, you are getting yourself back, finding yourself again."

I nod because I know what he means but I pretend I don't. "Okay, whatever," I say, and continue with my book.

Here's a secret. Since I have started writing with the purpose of eventually having readers myself, I have been scared to read another's work. I am scared that my thoughts have been printed many times before and are but used up notions, tattered and passed around far too often. I am scared that my story will be a disappointment, scared that I cannot articulate very well... and most of all I am scared that I will not meet Kim's expectations. She expected great things from me, as I expected great things from her, but I am giving it my all, I am really trying... And when I read something beautiful I cannot help but wish that I had written just that.

I am slowly beginning to realise, though, that it is about the emotion you put behind your pen, about just being you and going for it and not comparing yourself to another because each of us is unique and beauty always lies in an honest heart. Even if it is only a half-heart like mine. I guess I am scared that the world will not care what I have to say, and scared that Kim will not become a character whom people know about, and scared because writing feels like my whole life now. And if my written words are not validated then I, as a person, am also invalid.

THIRTEEN

AM I READY?

A m I ready to tell the truth - the truth that I have been abused and damaged by an evil man? The truth is that Otak disguised himself as something that he was not. He came over from Afghanistan and I fell, like the Border Agency fell, for his lies. We thought he had fled for his life. I thought he cared about me and that he had no-one other than me. The truth is that everything I thought about him when we became friends and I moved in with him was a complete lie. He was not the age he said he was, his family were not all dead and he did not love me. He was obsessed, but his obsession was dark and a million miles away from love.

He managed to slip under everybody's radar; he was a psychopath and his stories and behaviour throughout the relationship spelled that out very boldly though, by the time the cracks starting appearing in his act, I was trapped. He used to tell me that he wanted to be abducted by aliens because then he could eradicate the whole of humanity. He told me that he despised women, all but me. Yet still he managed to rape me, threaten me and violate my basic human rights endlessly. He dressed me up and told me to keep my head down whenever we were in public; later, my being in public, even if it was just the corner shop, became forbidden. He was my master.

I could not leave because he threatened to hurt those I cared about and I was not prepared to do this - until my survival instincts kicked in and I did leave in fear of my own life.

The truth is, there were many warning signs. But have you ever heard of a tragedy occurring and someone saying, "Well, guys, I saw that coming"? Of course not. Nobody sees it coming. I was never a girl whose sister was going to be murdered. I wasn't a girl who accepted abuse. Yet it happened. Kim was never a girl who would be murdered and nor was Sammy. They were both young, pretty starlets in the making in my eyes, yet they are now the girls who were murdered by my ex-boyfriend.

I look at Mel who is seated next to me on the bedside chair. "Don't let the truth hit me too hard, Mel. Do you think you could delete my past?" I ask.

"Don't try to delete it from your memory," he says. "If you delete your past completely, you delete the existence of the two most inspirational girls to have ever existed." And he holds my hand as I sob in a controlled manner.

Some minds are evil. Because of their brain chemistry, they cannot feel empathy and this combined with a poor upbringing could turn that person into an evil individual. Some minds are possessed by darkness and demons that will not leave and they slowly take that person and twist their hearts, which were not beating very well to begin with. They make the host like a demon that appears just like the rest of us. Yet these people do come as light-bringers into our lives, as co-dependants to us, and this was the case with the brute. They bring with them nothing but deception and they are fantastic illusionists.

I left hospital abruptly because I wasn't told in advance when I would get a flat of my own until just a few days before. I would like to say that I left gracefully but that would be a lie. I cried and I swore that I would send my sister after them. Then I left in a taxi with all my belongings to go and live temporarily in Marshway, a scruffy block of self-contained flats similar in style to a hostel, with members of staff on site at all hours and tenants who have clearly lost themselves in drugs and alcohol.

For a while I stayed in contact with patients from Fieldhead. Mel helped me with my belongings and slept with me in my new flat on the sofa, which was more appropriate for us to sleep on, and we played acoustic love songs whilst knocking ourselves out with sleepers and wishing our lives away. I will always struggle to keep my mind positive, but this is okay, I am adapting to it.

I kept this place up and kept my mental health in check for a while, until boredom set in and I sold my soul and my story to the media (who are employed by the devil) and lavished the money they paid out on material goods. Now, I know this is a pretty damn low thing to do. But please remember that I had just lost every-thing and when you have lost everything you will do anything and get anything. Mel was by my side as I spoke to the reporters; the trial had not been over with for long and he received a sentence of thirty-one years for double homicide - but this is not something I see any point in going into because it is just what it is.

Mainly with the money I received from various newspapers, I decided I needed to get out of Wakefield and out of the spotlight where I was pitied, hated or just constantly told how strong I was. I wanted so badly to be a person again, a person who is not linked to a horrific crime, a person who could smile without being told "Oh, you are so strong" or asked "But why didn't you stop him?" - a mindless and completely ludicrous thing to say, for no-one on this planet, even those with heart-breaking bravery, would have been able to stop him. I did my own research into the fight-or-flight response and discovered that it is natural for the brain to freeze when it can do neither.

Anyhow, I have no-one to prove myself to. I have never wished harm upon anyone and never intentionally done anything to hurt anyone. This is a good quality to have in this world and any judgements cast upon me are by sinful minds - and we all sin. Let the judgements be cast on Judgement Day and let's see where we all stand then; until then please don't judge a situation you have never been anywhere near to experiencing. I trust my readers are of a compassionate nature...

I visited the grave on one occasion and was accused of dancing upon it, because of a picture that went onto Facebook, which is full of bitchiness. Let me tell you, this accusation made me rage for it is an absurd, extremely hurtful and also a very low thing to say. But the woman who said it is one of those screwed-up characters so I guess such nasty things escape her loud mouth on a daily basis. I stopped visiting the grave somewhere along the lines. It was not the comment that stopped me but the way that the grave was now presented since my mother had managed to get the money together for a headstone. This headstone was a harsh wake-up call, for the words engraved upon it are of cold, hard stone, and the name of what once was a beating heart is now cold like the doll's head when her life had left her. And I now do not see any point in going to sit above a vessel, a dead, decaying corpse; this will not make me feel 'connected' to Kim in any way shape or form. I stressed this to my family earlier and they disagreed with my words, as people often do. But I speak them only believing the thought to be true. A grave is merely a display, and when I die I hope my relatives and friends will not visit me in such a morbid place, for sure as hell my spirit will not be hanging around in a graveyard. I'll be off floating through the ether, as light as air, probably smoking my favourite brand of cigarette that I couldn't afford before.

Planning the funeral seemed to me equally as pointless as the burial and visiting the grave. The flowers were arranged so very carefully and all I could think was, 'Kim doesn't give a fuck what flowers you pick'; in fact, deciding on the flower arrangements took a good few days of sitting around a table by relatives who were never there for me or Kim, discussing which colours symbolised what in relation to Kim. Sunflowers - why sunflowers? Did Kim like purple roses? Well, everybody likes roses, everybody likes romance and she liked the colour purple; but did she really like purple roses enough for them to 'symbolise' her? I doubt it, she was not a flowery kind of girl - she was pretty and had a beautiful personality, but she held higher regard for cigarettes and alcohol and good music and the symbolism of word phrases than she did for roses. She did like butterflies though, so I accept the way that people leave butterflies at her grave.

I guess some people are full of well-meant yet stupid sentiments and this becomes especially evident during funeral arrangements. Maybe they don't know what else to do so they fuss about insignificant things and apply meanings to them, on behalf of a person who is dead. Everything becomes about 'display' after death: we must keep the neatness of the grave to appropriate standards, we must make sure we are all so very finely attired in black, the wake must have carefully displayed finger foods and within a few weeks the house must become a photographic exhibition of the one who is deceased. Then after all this has passed, after a few weeks or months or years, then what is there left to do? Well, nothing but cry and find a way to appreciate the person's life through something other than 'display'.

Although I won't be seeing her grave again, I plan on setting up a shrine in some local woods for her. This is more apt. If I could have my way, I would have a statue of her built in London for tourists to come and stare at, to admire and to shed a tear or two for her – but no more because me and her never liked soppy people.

You may be wondering if I have received any therapy and bizarrely enough I have not. I have not talked to a single professional in depth about what happened. I receive therapy through my writing. And through Mel. But that is all. It has been a few years now and, believe me, what happened to me will never sink in. Yet I make the best out of what I have, and right now that is nothing other than a notebook I bought from the Pound Shop and a black biro, and these will take me away.

The surgeon was sadly sadistic,
all his work ritualistic,
he made his bride with patchwork pride,
the beauty of love's darker side.

He hated his bride, she was materialistic
and dolled herself up with ruby lipstick
and with putrid passion, he grew sick.

The surgeon saw love as purely sadistic
while his bride's eyes ran red, looking unrealistic,
and as she grew she went ballistic
for she knew it was true, she had to reside
in her maker's hands, with patchwork pride
as under his surgical smile, he chose to hide.

The 1812 Overture comes through the speakers in my Dad's room. I'm wearing a red beret and painting away with passion while my Dad is on his computer, writing with equal passion. The crescendo begins and our pace picks up with it, my brush flowing back and forth in a hurry as though the love I have for life is spilling over and pouring out as I see explosions of rich colour fill my canvas. I imagine it as Bonfire Night because that's coming up soon and when the fireworks explode into their patterns I become enthralled by them and wonder if I could set my heart alight and watch it take off and explode, showering down dust onto those below. And so I add a heart to my canvas.

My Dad turns to me and grins from under his baseball cap (one of many) as he waves his hands back and forth as though conducting with a smile spread across his face that speaks volumes. Tchaikovsky is running through my veins and I feel in the right place for once in my life and doing the right thing, creating.

I go back to my flat in Marshway every evening and write by candle light, not to romanticise the scene but because I can never afford electricity. And that's because I am an impulsive buyer and prioritise new shoes over staying warm in November; but I often keep the tags on clothing items in case I should need to bring them back when I have no electric or gas. Yes, I know I am a stupid girl. I then awake in the mornings, freezing and excited, get dressed as quickly as I can and make it to my Dad's for precisely 7.30 a.m. where he has a coffee and roll-up waiting for me. This is a daily routine but, unlike routine, it is exciting.

At these times, my Dad's neighbours on the top floor of the Talbot and Falcon, the Irish pub where he lives, are subject to our musical tastes which range from classical to System Of A Down and varies as much as our moods. More than likely though, Jake Bugg will be playing for us; my Dad's hero, he helps us to write and he is also quite cute. For a man in his mid-fifties, my Dad has an awesome taste in music, in fact he's the only person I know whose taste cannot be insulted. Half Man Half Biscuit, Bob Dylan and Joni Mitchell are among his favourites while writing. My Mum is also very much into music but with somewhat different tastes, and sometimes I miss her and the music she would play.

Me and my Dad have spent the last week making up our own songs in which I usually sing some Taylor Swift-style lyrics but in my head pretend I'm Courtney Love image-wise and I strain my voice to hit notes it will never reach. My Dad plays guitar as Mr Bean films us. He lives two rooms down from my Dad and, guess what, resembles Rowan Atkinson, hence his nickname. He does a perfect impression of the real Mr Bean too and the whole town refers to him this way, much to his dislike though he has grown to accept it. I have never laughed so hard as when I am round here, with these guys.

"Hey, Beanie," I say as my Dad lets Mr Bean in. They get together every morning and have smokes before they set about the day. Occasionally they have to copper up for a few cans. They are merry drinkers. Mr Bean scowls and then smiles, a genuine smile.

"You still singing that Tobias song?" he says jokingly, humming to my pathetic attempt at romance.

"Yep, I am. Are you still singing it while working?" I fire back at him.

"Aye, I am," he says. He always has happy eyes.

And I probably look silly sitting there with my ambitious eyes and a paint brush in my hand, but this is what it's all about, I think, as I continue painting and Mr Bean makes roll-ups for us all. I find it kind of funny but try not to smile as my Dad and Mr Bean raid a pint glass that stands on top of the TV; they have 66 pence in coppers and Mr Bean empties his pockets to make up the rest. What I find funny is the way we all go about our day with empty pockets, just living, smiling penniless smiles that get us by. And sometimes that's all we want.

At this point I realise something I should have known all along - I can be happy again and I don't have to worry about being happy alone. I have a chance and I don't need to do anything right now other than be me. I don't need grandiose ideas to keep me perked up, nor do I need to obsess over guys. I don't need to diet until I become weak, I just need to do what I am doing right now and everything will fall into place. It has to. It's the law of attraction.

Later in the day, my Dad has made some cash from selling his DVDs and Mr Bean has finished his shift, so we all go downstairs to the bar. I do not drink, I just become merry around the people who do drink here. It's a spirited place and everybody's spirits are high, raising mine each time I enter. Nigel stands at the bar.

"Hey up, DVD," he says to my Dad as he slumps his bag onto the floor. Nigel is the landlord of the Talbot and he's a star. He helped out my Dad and David during those dark hours after the death of Kim, drove them to the funeral and financially supported them. Nigel met Kim when she and I sat at a table a year ago as self-declared vegetarians who happened to eat pie and peas. People here are actual real characters, like ones you could have pulled out of a book or a film, characters you remember.

These are the days that I know I'll remember for as long as forever lasts. If I die tomorrow, I can say I have experienced happiness and because of this I also feel sorrow. I have broken my vow to Kim, betrayed her in a way I cannot explain. So I beg her not to pay me any visits at night. No reminders, please, I say to myself.

I walk back to Marshway. I wanted to stay at my Dad's but Mel is at my flat waiting for me to return so we can lie down on the sofa together and tell each other fairy tales with our own twists. We hope that one day we can live one out, in a different lifetime. But for now we find pleasure in pain and we recognise our narcissistic needs for the world to shower us with condolences. Then the stars will shine and illuminate all that we are; and even if what we are is nothing, under starlight we become everything.

"Are you sure we can do this?" I turn and say to my Dad as we sit with a display of framed felt-tip pictures on Whitby Bay, the sand inbetween my toes.

"We can," he says, hiding his can of Carling behind the rucksack. I see faith in his eyes and I believe him, that we can be somebodies. We have our writing and we are pursuing that, and now we have my art work, which is mainly a collection of drawings of zombies and weird abstract ideas, that we are determined will work.

We have been in Whitby a good few weeks now and we are staying with a man we met in a pub; my brother came too but he left to go back to Wakefield when the money ran out and being a person who possesses common sense he realised this was a crazy idea. The man we are staying with is called Ty and he has a dog that I dislike strongly; it is a Japanese Akita and is very sloppy, licking its paws that have sores all over them. Ty is just a guy we met in a pub called The Ship and we immediately got talking to him because my Dad had put one of my pastel drawings on the table, which attracted the guy's attention. We were staying in a cottage at first but with the money gone we thought we'd have to return to Wakefield, back to the small town where nothing ever happens. We told Ty about our dilemma and he offered to let us stay at his flat overlooking Whitby Bay and the small town.

Now, I am sitting on a rock with my pictures before me for the entire world to see. A young couple with children by their side walk over – it is the school holidays – and they seem enthusiastic as I say "Hello" until they look down and the enthusiasm melts into mild disgust. The zombies and dying brides do not impress them, or their children for that matter. "Very nice," they say half-heartedly, then stroll off.

"Dad," I say, "nobody likes them."

"I think they do, dear," he replies, trying to hold in a little laugh. "It's just that they might be a bit too gory for them, especially when they've got kids. You know what I mean, Lace?"

I let out a little laugh. "Yeah, I guess we should have thought about the school holidays and what audience the pictures would be presented to." He laughs too as he takes a swig from his can. "Shall we try going somewhere else to sell them?" I suggest, and we both laugh and begin packing up. I am wearing my multi-coloured tie-dye jacket and the trilby hat which has become my staple clothing item this summer. "We could try on the abbey steps?" I ask.

"Yes, dear."

We go up the hundred steps to the abbey. The charming cobbled streets are bustling with people but we make our way there and all I can think of to myself is how happy I am. When we reach the top of the steps we decide to sit at the edge of the abbey facing towards the spooky-looking castle, which is just past the graveyard. My Dad sets the pictures out, taking four different designs and standing them up against the stone we are sitting on. We have priced them at £15 each and considered that reasonable, but people's faces are disagreeing; in fact most people are walking right past us or almost falling over us because of the angle we are sitting at, just sat there like lemons.

"Have we picked another bad spot?" I say.

"We have. People can't see us 'til they turn the corner so all we're doing is making people jump," my Dad says light-heartedly and again we laugh in unison. "Don't worry, we'll get there eventually," he says as he rolls us both a cigarette and I believe him. Eventually we find a spot at the bottom of the steps and set up third time lucky, next to a man who is selling jet. Many people walk by us and take a look but it is only ever a very brief look; I am not disheartened by this at all though, not in the least, and the reason is because I can tell by my Dad's face that he believes in me.

We leave that day but we won't stop, we won't give in because we have Kim on our side and fuck the rest of the world. We will become somebodies. My Dad is creative genius and I guess I've picked up some of his creative genes.

Pump acrylic through my veins,
cement the moment with a wish
to die with artistic remains
and the love of another's pain.
Paint me up in vivid colours,
paint a rainbow over this town
before I expire
of artless desire
or die of the will to inspire.
Another dying day
of blooded brushes that decay.
The day you went away I heard
your spirit saying, "Soothe me please,"
on your knees,
yearning to become a picture
that I desire to see,
the picture of you and me.

We have just arrived back from London and GMTV was a disaster beyond belief. Mel journeyed with me and my Dad - he has been staying in Whitby too and he helps me and my Dad promote my art work, which is now on display in a few different shops. We decided to go on the This Morning programme to tell my tale, but most importantly to promote my art, and naïve as we were it didn't happen how we had anticipated. The media are only interested in the grisly details and they do not care about whether they provoke emotions in you as they ask for vivid recollections.

Now with money in the bank again, me and my Dad decided we needed a car as things were really looking up for us. We had an art exhibition lined up at the upcoming Dracula Festival; they had accepted us and to exhibit my art there. We bought ourselves arty clothes and spent hours taking shadowy photographs during misty mornings up by the castle ruins and on the beach. We put our souls into this and we were moving on. We had left everything behind in Wakefield and made many people angry because of our contact with the media, but people do not see things logically, their opinions always tainted by painful emotions. Me and my Dad were doing all of this for Kim. We were ruthless but if you want to be successful in life you have to be; the only time emotions are put to good use is through the arts.

I went to the hairdresser's in Whitby town centre and Mel kept me company there, bringing me numerous coffees and science magazines because he knows I do not like the usual fashion magazines. My Dad and Ty arrived not long after I got back to the flat. Ty had ordered some charlie and now wanted £200 so I handed it to him; I felt we deserved a good time after all our hard work, although drugs are not really my thing. We spent the night using my new art materials, sitting and chatting as I scruffily spread various pastels across my canvases. I got my Dad to do some drawing and Ty drew a tree that was a complete failure in life.

Later we went for a drive and the lights of Whitby's street lamps talked to me, telling me, "Hey you, I thought you were a somebody now?" I burst out laughing and took my camera out so I could record every moment. The charming cobbled roads wound like a small maze and I pictured my mind as a maze with Mel chasing me down it until my head hurt, so we stopped at a pub and had a beer. I became afraid of a comedown but it didn't happen, and we fell asleep at 2 a.m. sober, yet wired.

We woke up groggily and shut the sunlight away, closing the curtains quickly. I was on a blow-up bed on the floor and my Dad was on the sofa. We didn't like these sleeping arrangements but we planned to move out of there into a nice big house, with a giant study each and all the equipment necessary for an artist such as myself. Kim used to tell me to get myself to college when I was sixteen and to pursue an art career. We used to draw pictures for each other. The last one I drew for her was of a white tiger with inspirational quotes around it, hoping to lift her out of the depression she was then in. Me and my Dad, we were holding on to this dream and it felt just around the corner, so we spent the next few days sitting in various pubs and displaying my art work on beer garden tables, with still not a single buyer. We took the occasional boat trip with sailor Sam, a ginger guy with a huge beard who drove a boat and had a crush on me, and our evenings we spent joking and laughing out loud about characters we had invented until stupid hours. We wrote and we tried to promote me as much as possible.

In the meantime Ty was becoming greedy and ordering more charlie, which I ended up paying for again… and again… and again. And I ended up sleeping with Ty after one drunken night in the pub. I was now becoming uncomfortable with the whole living arrangement so my pictures became gorier and my mind slowly unravelled with each line.

"Do you think Ty is taking the piss out of us?" I asked my Dad one night when Ty was out, and my Dad nodded.

"It will be okay. Just hang on until I make you a star and we'll be outta here," and I felt better right away. But I didn't feel better for long and I was slowly doubting myself more and more as each day went by, until one evening I walked up to the top of the Crocodile Cliff, ready to join the ship wrecks. All of sudden, as I was closing my eyes and feeling the wind, Mel touched my shoulder.

"You know that's a stupid thing to do," he said.

"But Mel, I feel like I'm fooling myself. I feel like a liar. Who am I fooling? I'm a nobody, a Whitby coke whore," I said.

"No, you're not. You are Lacey Jayne and your Dad's view of you is accurate - you are a star. You're a star to those who matter, you're a star in my eyes, you're a star in your Dad's eyes, and in Faye's eyes you're a star. Faye is still young and she's already lost one sister. David needs a sister. You need to stay, Elisa. We all need you, your mother included," he said. And because Mel is always honest, I thought for a second and then took a few steps back and plonked myself on the ground with my head in my hands.

"I'm so scared, Mel," I said. "I'm scared to continue living. I'm scared I can't make it."

"You already have made it, to those around you. You did a brave thing coming out here, you and your Dad both, you took a chance. Most people don't take chances, they play it safe and they miss out on the moments like you and your Dad have been having - and will continue to have."

I lifted my hands from my face and wiped my nose on Mel's sleeve. When I stood up he wiped my tears and held my hand, leading me back to Ty's house, then he kissed me goodnight and told me he was going back to Wakefield. I fell asleep and woke up to a morning sun that penetrated my soul and I felt like a lost child without Mel being in Whitby. So this is when I decided to go back to Wakefield, this is when I let mine and my Dad's dreams fall out of reach, this is when I let Kim down. The seaside mourned for us when we left, but we will be back one day.

The little girl sat there drawing,
not really thinking or knowing
is this painting good enough.
Then God descended from above…

Yes it is.

Sorted, by Paul Stephens

FOURTEEN

WHERE IS MEL?

Where, oh where, is my darling Mel? It's been weeks now and I am dying of loneliness. I miss the way he speaks, the way he whispered to me under the blankets in Fieldhead. I miss his quirky style and the way he smiles when he speaks of the things he loves, such as late nights and Venice or other parts of Italy. I miss the stories he told and I even miss his irritating habits, like when he talks over me, or kisses me when I need it though I tell him not to touch me because I don't want comforting, yet he comforts me anyway. I miss our morning walks when the weather is cold and the streets are empty and frosty. I miss the nights we laid under the stars and wished ourselves dead, but only because we were bored. I miss his sarcasm and I miss having his constant wit and humour and actually understanding it. Without him I lose everything, I lose any barriers between myself and the world, between myself and others. Why did he leave me? He cannot leave me - I created him!

Mel was the kind of guy who could charm the pants off anyone and disarm the coldest of hearts, finding something buried deep down inside them, like the loss of a loved one, and making this pain and loss feel comforting in nature. Mel once told me that he would marry me if he wasn't fictional - this made me laugh at the time, but I wish I hadn't laughed because I want to get married some day. I want to become stable enough to love another and Mel has been a friend and companion for some time now, so we could have got married. I never figured that I would ache without him.

Time stands still now that he is gone and I feel the world might swallow me whole, because what am I without him? I miss his OCD nature and his soft lips, which I never kissed all that often because we kissed through lines of stories. And now I wish I'd kissed him for real. I cannot get through my days without him, so I cry and cry and I weep myself to sleep; and, in a way that I have never felt before, I miss my mother and it's her that I want. I call out to her and fall apart as I lay my head down.

I have had four hospital admissions since Fieldhead, all after the Whitby excursion. I guess when you're busy there aren't so many hours to have breakdowns. But I have just managed to get myself a flat that is concrete and I will be in there for at least six months; I have made it into a spiritual haven. I am spending this afternoon in Prêt, my favourite coffee house, and I'm writing a new poem for a shaman who is a good friend as of recent - we have a bit of a thing going on at the minute. He is teaching me about magic and things that I used to know. I struggle, listening to people's gossiping tongues, idle gossip; I am learning mindfulness so this helps when I feel myself becoming agitated by mindless gossip.

A man is standing outside leaning against W H Smith where a lady often shows up busking and he's staring me out. 'What a creep,' I think. He has been watching me here every day for a while, the last fortnight without missing me once. I put my journal away and get up to leave and go to confront the man. He looks a bit similar to Mel. I saw Mel passing by in the city centre with a bouquet of flowers in his hand the other week and when I tried to catch up with him I lost him; the flowers were purple roses though, so I know where he was heading. I step out of the coffee shop and am nearly knocked over by a tall, scary-looking man. Then I look over at the creepy man whose face I cannot see; he takes his hood down... and it is Mel!

"Mel!" I shout, running towards him as a few people whom I push past tut at me. His boyish charm is as evident as ever.

"Lacey Jayne!" he says, holding his arms out. I run and jump up into them, wrap my arms and legs around him and he spins me around. As he puts me down I realise that my fifties-style cupcake dress has lifted in the wind so I tug it down. I kiss Mel and he kisses me back.

"Where the heck have you been?" I ask, giddily.

He takes my hand. "Come, let's go sit down and talk." We sit in a beer garden at The Packhorse pub. It is empty and I am thankful because craziness is a thing of the past for me, at least, that's what I want you to believe. I go and buy two Malibus and Cokes and it tastes nice and sweet. "I never wanted to leave you before, Elisa," he says as I play with my straw, wondering if the old days are back.

"It's Lacey now," I butt in.

"Okay, Lacey." He pulls out an e-cig and has a quick blast of it. "I never wanted to leave you, but you left me with no choice. By God, I have missed you though."

Mel came into my dreams after I saw him with the purple roses; he told me I should visit my sister's grave. Now I feel a pain resurrect in me.

"Me too, but I just couldn't do it, Mel, I couldn't go to the grave. I couldn't stay in Whitby and you shouldn't have left me without a single letter or `phone call."

"I know, I know." He looks affectionate and his eyes water slightly.

"How long are you in town for?" I ask casually.

He looks at his wrist watch. "Not long, in fact I only called by to see how you were."

I become disenchanted. "Yeah, I'm good. You know, same old…" and my voice trails off as I look away.

"I saw you with a hippy-looking guy a few days ago. I've been watching you. But I didn't want to come and talk to you when you were in company."

"Yeah, that was Dylan," I say, hoping he is happy for me. "We're not seeing each other or anything but, you know, we enjoy each other's company. We met at an acoustic night," I say, grinning accidently.

"Well, if he makes you happy that's all that matters."

"I guess it is."

"But please, do something for me - go to visit your sister's grave in your dreams."

"I will." I take a long drag of my cigarette and blow the smoke out. "I will." And, just this once, I mean it.

"Good. Well, now I know you're good I'd best be on my way."

"What? You're going to leave me just like that, all over again?" I say.

"Elisa, whenever I leave you it's going to be hard. You're in love with me, aren't you?" he asks. "You're in love with me because I'm your own sadness personified and you need me because you're afraid to be happy."

"I know, I know," I say and my throat closes up. "Then what about your half a heart?" I ask. "Do you not want the half you lent me back?"

"I can get by on half a heart."

"But what about me? When we're together we have a full beating heart." My words come out involuntarily and my heart is clenched with some kind of angry offshoot.

"Don't you see? Dylan has already given you a quarter of his heart, for keeps. And there's Adam and your family and the other people you've come across, the people who have felt something for you over the past year and a half. You have a complete heart now. It may not have the same anatomy as other people's but it's yours. So now go out and feel as much as you can with it."

"Okay... but will I ever see you again?" I ask, as I fight back tears and the sky becomes slightly stormy. Kim dislikes people abandoning me.

"Of course you will, you can call on me whenever you want. I won't be far away," Mel says. He begins walking away and people are looking at me as if I am crazy, but I don't care. I run after Mel and hug him.

"I missed you so much. I always will."

"We will meet again." And that goes without saying, we both know this, and it's nice to listen to his heart beating just for a few minutes. Then he leaves. I watch him merge into the crowd of people, the crowd that I will never be a part of because I have a different kind of heart to theirs. This is fine with me.

The End

I am happy with this end. It is not a fairy tale ending but life never imitates fairy tale endings and this is the closest it will ever be to that for me. But that doesn't mean we cannot have fairy tale chapters dotted throughout our lives, and this is what I look forward to. Mel and Kim are my fairy tale heroes who will create these chapters for me, and I just have to keep my pen ready... always ready.

FIFTEEN
A POSTSCRIPT

By Mel

I am very relevant in this story. I am Elisa's best friend and sometimes I am her lover too. I came about through careful creation due to a beautiful imagination, grief and Elisa's predisposition to depression. I have been to Hell and back with Elisa. I have witnessed her nightmares and, let me tell you, they kill her inside. You know, she can't be a real dreamer anymore because PTSD nightmares have etched themselves and their evil essence deeply into her brain. She cannot have pastel dreams in shades of pink and blue anymore, only hard, vivid shades of red. Most of the time her dreams offer nothing but blood-red rage directed at the girl who was once her sister. How could she be her sister? She was just the ghost of a murdered girl. She ceased to exist, Elisa told me. I then asked Elisa to question existence itself and she will eventually realise a thing or two.

Even if her nightmares are not directly set in 'the event', as she refers to it, they are either sad orchestrations of her own suicide or dreams laced with a deeply buried guilt she hides away in waking hours. But she has ability, she can daydream. She can dream her way through life and I trust, now I am not around for her anymore, that this is what she will do. She will write and paint and sing as though she is not in this realm. And she will cry and die inside sometimes, but she will get through it; and if she doesn't, I shall be there to hold her and whisper in her ear all the things she needs to hear, such as "Stuff the world" or "Fuck them all".

What am I? I am melancholy. I am the grey areas in life. I am the sadness that dwells within her forever and always. I am the sadness one feels when gazing out, through double-glazed windows that do nothing to keep out winter's chill, at a grey sky with fading clouds heavy not with rainwater but with teardrops that have been cried by broken-hearted angels. I am the woodland with creeping, leafless trees that ache and moan, longing for summer. I am everything that is pleasurable only under a certain light, that daylight when the sun has temporarily expired.

You'll look around and see me in the faces of others. I am so very beautiful that in fact I shock myself when I see my own reflection. I am rather dashing and I use this to lead others into a reckless abandon of mind, body and soul. For Elisa, I was a dark and disgraceful wonder that held her as she rocked back and forth in her hospital gown, praying to turn back time's wicked hands, praying to make just one single decision different.

And I sat with her as she scribbled down her thoughts.

I met her sister a few times because I often showed up in Elisa's nightmares, just to let her know that if Otak turned up I would handle it - I would instantaneously lose my shit, disarm him and then comfort Elisa, Kim and Sammy. I sat with Elisa as she made her way around the world, trying to find a safe place to cry after the event. She did find respite in Fieldhead, and friendships that she will keep within her messed-up heart for the rest of her days.

Months after her leaving Fieldhead, she ended up back in hospital. This time she was placed in a hospital in Halifax, on Elmdale Ward, because Fieldhead was full at the time. When she was first admitted to Elmdale, she swore she had contracted mind sickness again and had yielded to its ravenous destruction of the mind and body. This is to say, she was deeply depressed and had become sick through breathing in the air of Wakefield town centre, polluted by toxic words and unhappy faces, an air that poisons your lungs if you try to breathe in life. Elisa became so laden with remorse and an overwhelming fear of death that she threw red paint all over the walls of her new flat in a desperate attempt to recreate her nightmares for all to see. She then took an overdose, neither wishing to live nor die, and was taken into the general infirmary where the nurses put her on a drip. Overdose was becoming rather routine to her by now, so she complied and was then booked onto Elmdale Ward where she was welcomed in the same way that Fieldhead had done.

But then this experience was a whole different one for Elisa. I sat with her as she cried in her hospital bedroom, standing in the middle of the room and running her hands through her hair, in a long NHS hospital gown that was oversized and made her appear small and defenceless from the world that normal people live in. And when she cried I thought it would never end. She could not speak this time and she did not make friends, though she did make a few scenes. On one occasion as I was sitting with her in her bedroom, I prompted her to sit with the others in the small main lounge. She did so but sat with her headphones in so she wouldn't have to communicate with the others, remaining reserved for as long as she could. I was reading the magazines that were spread across a large central table. Then a guy walked in with curly brown hair and asked her to dance, to which Elisa agreed (going bright red - it was such a cute moment). He twirled her around and then asked her out on a date and she responded, "Of course." When we went back to her room we had a discussion and I told her never to give her heart so freely to anyone as she had done in the past.

She recorded video diaries each day that told of her inner suffering, which life beyond the hospital walls never saw. Her demeanour always had a 'keeping it together' quality - keeping it together but invisibly expiring. Now, my demeanour is melancholic, though hopefully never grumpy since grumpy people need shooting. She was always seen as strong or even indifferent by some ignorant minds. All of that unravelled and it was very evident to her brother David that she was secretly heavily affected, in a way that the world could never comprehend. Her own worst enemy. She then took drugs that a patient's father had sneaked onto the ward, and another time when a patient's friend had delivered cocaine disguised in a take-away box.

After only a week on the ward, Elisa was told that she would be discharged within another week and this scared her, so she begged for some extra time but this was refused. She told me she could not bear people's prying eyes as she went about her daily life, in clothes that were not as black as death. (Personally I am usually attired in black and I told Elisa she should wear black more often as it is a slimming colour, but she took offence.) So she prolonged her hospital stay by acting out in a psychotic fashion, because patients with psychotic illnesses receive more compassion from the nurses than patients with personality disorders; the nurses forget that these people have usually been through very traumatic experiences, and regard people with personality disorders as neither sane nor insane.

This is what Elisa did. She stood still in the middle of the corridor late one night as patients sat around chattering to one another. A member of staff asked her if she was okay and she replied with a face of feigned sincerity, "I am going to set myself on fire." Then she pulled her lighter from her leather jacket pocket and predictably two nurses grabbed hold of her as she kicked and screamed "Lucifer!" at the top of her voice. It screeched right through me and sent a shiver down my spine as

I stood watching in amazement. She cried hysterically and began trying to bang her head on the floor, and I looked into her eyes as two nurses dragged her into the isolation room. She looked the stereotypical crazy lady. I couldn't recognise her for a few seconds, her eyes were different and in this moment it was obvious that she really was mentally unwell. She continued screeching in the isolation room, pulling at her hair and scratching herself repeatedly in an attempt to become 'officially crazy' so she could stay on the ward longer.

Although this was all supposedly staged - that's what she told me the following day - when I looked at her through the small window of the isolation room I saw the truth. I saw a purist, I saw her as an artist creating one's own madness. However it was not completely staged: the ceaseless tears and random laughing were her real self, slightly dramatised, but the banshee wails were real. She told the nurses to leave her alone and then sat rocking back and forth, looking jittery, whispering harshly and telling 'the voices' to shut up. Later she would sit with wild eyes, revealing a desperate need to be helped, flitting from face to face of the concerned nurses. Then she swallowed a sedative, stopped her absurd ranting and when the nurses left she smiled.

"Elisa, you are going to get better, I swear it, okay? You have one hell of a guardian angel," I said to her that same night. She giggled as though sarcastically amused and eventually reached a point where her emotions became dampened and apathy set in once more.

"Don't let the world swallow me whole. Don't let my night-mares take me," she replied, as I cradled her to sleep. There was the sound of scampering outside as the night-time creatures came out to play and trick the minds of unstable patients. I remained silent throughout the night and prayed that this was not the end of me or of her.

The following morning she sat and wrote in her journal to Kim, and then as I ate my toast in the school-like dining room she went out and bought us a bottle of wine to share. She sneaked it onto the hospital ward and, although I strongly disapproved of her drinking, she was unstoppable and impulsive so I couldn't really intervene. I also couldn't tell the nurses because no-one can see me. We had a heart to heart and I saw her as she really was, with no pretence, no act. Mind sickness can strip us of our defences, you see. She played The Smiths' Asleep over and over and I prayed to Kim to sprinkle down some angel dust. So she did, though it came not in the form of actual fairy dust but recreational drugs, charlie. Elisa sniffed it up and was told by the nurses that the doctor would be coming to see her and maybe she would be sectioned.

"Oh God, no - I can't be sectioned!" she replied theatrically, while secretly feeling rather pleased about this possible decision.

"Elisa, you can't see the doctor as you are now," I told her, as she stood staring at her gaunt mirror image in her bedroom, her bloodshot eyes telling of recent binge and purge cycles.

"Mel, I can do what I want. I'm a fucking disgrace and I no longer care," she replied.

"No, you are not," I said as I spun her round. I wiped the eyeliner that had become smudged, patted the stray strands of her blissful blonde hair down and wondered where my girl had gone. She just laughed to herself and her eyes were vacant of the personality she once had, one of innocence, charm and softness. It surely is mind sickness, I thought.

The doctor saw her and she told him, "I am going to kill you." She jumped on the filing cabinets and laughed manically, telling the doctor she had the forces of Lucifer within her; this time she appeared to believe it completely and it shocked a few of the nurses. She didn't remember it the following day; in fact, her memory had become the jumble sale of memories that an old, crazy lady has, not that of a young girl with an organised mind but of a confused, wreckage of a mind that cannot arrange thoughts in an orderly way. I sat at her side and she kept telling me that time had become much distorted recently, that it had no line. A Section Two was imposed.

"Nicely done," I said to her, feeling annoyed that she was not fighting to become better.

She recovered from these episodes of mind sickness mixed with depressive mania and was released after three months of on-and-off psychotic events and tantrums. With a new medication she then re-entered the normal world, feeling like a new soul. I observed her making an attempt to live in this external world without a single clue about how to be someone who could fit into society without Kim's help or my own.

As I write this, I am sitting on a bench in the centre of Leeds, the city of hidden magic. It is full of trolls and a separate species of society known as the underclass, the tramps; one walks by me and I feel pity for him, yet he has the greatest smile one could ever see. I have been watching Elisa from afar recently while abiding with the rest of the dregs of society in a place known as The Crypt, a homeless shelter just by the hospital where Elisa has also stayed. She stopped receiving the help and the shelter that she needed after numerous hospitalisations, and when she presented at A & E the last time they told her to go to The Crypt. This charming little place (I am being sarcastic) is filled with all the kinds of people that a young girl should not be around. It has fifteen rooms and is part of an old building that is haunted by vengeful ghosts. There are no windows in the bedrooms and the shower areas stink of stale piss.

Elisa cried that first night. She cried in the shower as she looked at the mouldy ceiling and washed in the cold water that sprinkled down onto her face and neck. And, hitting reality, she sat in the corner beside the shower head and wished she were dead, for the world had really not offered any help in her distress. Besides me, and she held onto me, sweating in the hot and empty room. She cried for her sister and her mother. She told me that she had never needed her mother as an adult, but how she did that daunting night. She told me that everything in her life changed from one moment to the next and it was making her sick and dizzy. I said that this is just life and we have no choice but to accept it and that one day we will all be but dust and this is not a bad thing for then we will become one with our Creator. I didn't know what I meant by this but it's okay to be unsure and nobody has all the answers.

I came back here to The Crypt because I have to stick around in Leeds for a little while longer, to smile at the corrupt souls who are given beds here and who take advantage of unfortunate young girls who are thoughtlessly placed here by various services. One girl, a young Chinese woman, is in a room a few doors from my own and she's here because she is running away from incest and abuse. A man in a wheelchair saw her and, like the dog that he is, attempted to get some action from this poor helpless woman, who resisted him and spent the whole night praying to the Lord. Later, I went into the man's bedroom and felt utter hatred towards him, a man who deserved no life ahead of him. I now observe closely from the shadows where I am bound, because I am nothing and everything. Contradiction is everywhere in all things.

And, painstakingly, I watch through the crystal ball of my mind, as a broken girl begins to form new relationships. I watch my darling Elisa's heart fall in love again, watch her hurting eyes and convulsing heart as a guy whom she very much loves touches her, then hear her cry at 3 a.m. because he has turned against her. He has told that her he hates her and that she is a prude and that he has been so very patient with her. She has fallen apart, on her living room floor with cuts all over her arms and the crimson trickling down her pale skin. She is wearing a mask. She hates herself. And he has confirmed that she will never love again because she hasn't the capacity in this new heart of hers to feel love. He has left her and I know he is so very wrong; it is not that she cannot feel love, but she cannot give it back because she is a perfect example of a borderline's difficulty with intimacy.

They all leave her and she knows this is the way it has to be. She knows she is damaged and I wish I could pick her up and change her, for her sake; but from my melancholic point of view it makes her a beautiful person. She cannot be touched, cannot receive or give love to another except me and only me. Her guy sees her as being selfish and cold. Yes, she is cold but behind her sometimes absent eyes are vital signs of life, of the need to feel loved and to love as she had in the past when her heart was in its child-like naivety. Her guy has told her she is superficial, a fantasist and nothing but plastic. Sometimes she convinces herself of this too. So now she is stroking her kittens and telling them that love is for losers.

I must do something about this so I get out of my bed in The Crypt and decide it is time to pay her a visit. I will give her an idea, which is that maybe when she has shared her pain with the world through her writing then maybe it will be understood and she will know that the world is not bad. It's dark now and I walk in the centre of the road between the yellow lines that lead me to the one I love. I ring her doorbell and she answers with a bloody face and arms. The Eagles' Desperado is coming through her speakers. She looks at me as though she has been expecting me; her weeping eyes light up subtly and the corners of her mouth lift slightly. She invites me in and we begin to fix things, just for tonight. We will be okay someday. How? We are dreamers.

We sit and have late night coffee and cigarettes, which I roll carefully as I listen to her insistent ranting about being incapable of providing love for another. I ask her why and she says that love does not meet her expectations because a lover's love is not unconditional. Even if the boundaries are set low and conditions are placed wisely, that it is still conditional. I ask her if she wants companionship, the sort she had with her sister, a bond that is unconditional, and she tells me that this is all she wants and more than anything. And when I probe further, being a little analytical so I can confirm why she still keeps me around, she looks at her watch ignoring my thoughts and states with a harsh stare that she wants to stop delving into these notions of love and loss. So I drop it and tell her not to be afraid to love again because love is what makes the world go round, and surprisingly she doesn't dismiss this as hippy bullshit. Instead, she smiles knowingly and says, "I know, Mel." With her head down now, she rubs her forehead and leads me into the bedroom where we come undone and sink into her mattress, the sheets shielding us from the clawing shadows that hide among the furniture.

I cannot add much to this story now because I have my own demons that I must see to. I am friends with the shadows of people's pasts and I spend more time being nostalgic than thinking of the future. Like Elisa, I shall stick to being a dreamer. So I peck her now rosy cheek then go about my business doing what I do best, sitting in morbid places with a wistful look on my face and watching the world go by.

SIXTEEN

THE TRUTH AS I SEE IT

By Paul Stephens

Most things in life are not worth bothering about.
People die, don't ask me why, but these things happen.
And sometimes it's for the best.
Or is it?

Now this might seem intense, but the truth is not very often told,
so now I am going to tell you how things really were.

A princess had a beautiful little sister called Kimberley.
Now one day the God of Death took Kimberley
away from her elder sister.
How was the princess to react to this?
Her brother David had to go through all this too.
And what was he supposed to do?

Well she coped, as he did too.
And do you know why she got through all this dismay?
Because she was strong and loved her sister,
so naturally she was strong for her, as was her brother.

Now obviously they had a father and a mother.
The father wasn't there when he should have been,
but this would not have changed anything.
Destiny called that day and it did not matter anyway.

The big sister loved both parents, and so did Kimberley,
but they got so mixed up in the early years that their minds
became damaged before they had a chance to form.
The father was unaware of the early years
and had he known he would have been full of tears.

But there is no blame on anyone, except the guy who did the deed.

You can't turn back a clocked that's stopped.
And the dark is always brighter at night.

For Elisa and Dafydd

IF YOU HAVE ENJOYED THIS BOOK...

Local Legend is committed to publishing the very best spiritual writing, both fiction and non-fiction. You might also enjoy:

RAINBOW CHILD
S L Coyne (ISBN 978-1-907203-92-3)

Beautifully written in language that is alternately lyrical and childlike, this is the story of young Rebekah and the people she discovers as her family settles in a new town far from their familiar home. As dark family secrets begin to unravel, her life takes many turns both delightful and terrifying as the story builds to a tragic and breathless climax that just keeps on going. This book shows us how we look at others who are 'different'. Through the eyes of Rebekah, writing equally with passion and humour, we see the truth of human nature...

SPINACH SOUP FOR THE WALLS
Lynne Harkes (ISBN 978-1-907203-46-6)

Gold Medal Winner in the national *Wishing Shelf Book Awards*, this is a message of hope for anyone in despair. When we see our troubles as opportunities for growth, we can turn our lives around and "recognise the remarkable in the ordinary". Lynne has lived in many wonderful and colourful places, from South America to the jungle of Gabon in West Africa, and she describes graphically the resilience of the native peoples and the magnificence of the natural world. Yet she found herself retreating into unhappiness and isolation. This beautifully written book is the story of how she fought to rediscover her own spirituality and find a new way of thinking.

A SINGLE PETAL
Oliver Eade (ISBN 978-1-907203-42-8)

Winner of the national Local Legend *Spiritual Writing Competition*, this page-turner is a novel of murder, politics and passion set in ancient China. Yet its themes of loyalty, commitment and deep personal love are every bit as relevant for us today as they were in past times. The author is an expert on Chinese culture and history, and his debut adult novel deserves to become a classic.

AURA CHILD
A I Kaymen (ISBN 978-1-907203-71-8)

One of the most astonishing books ever written, telling the true story of a genuine Indigo child. Genevieve grew up in a normal London family but from an early age realised that she had very special spiritual and psychic gifts. She saw the energy fields around living things, read people's thoughts and even found herself slipping through time, able to converse with the spirits of those who had lived in her neighbourhood. This is an uplifting and inspiring book for what it tells us about the nature of our minds.

5P1R1T R3V3L4T10N5
Nigel Peace (ISBN 978-1-907203-14-5)

With descriptions of more than a hundred proven prophetic dreams and many more everyday synchronicities, the author shows us that, without doubt, we can know the future and that everyone can receive genuine spiritual guidance for our lives' challenges. World-renowned biologist Dr Rupert Sheldrake has endorsed this book as "...vivid and fascinating... pioneering research..." and it was national runner-up in *The People's Book Prize* awards.

THE QUIRKY MEDIUM
Alison Wynne-Ryder (ISBN 978-1-907203-47-3)

Alison is the co-host of the TV show *Rescue Mediums*, in which she puts herself in real danger to free homes of lost and often malicious spirits. Yet she is a most reluctant medium, afraid of ghosts! This is her amazing and often very funny autobiography, taking us 'back stage' of the television production as well as describing how she came to discover the psychic gifts that have brought her an international following. Winner of the Silver Medal in the national *Wishing Shelf Book Awards*.

These titles are all available as paperbacks and eBooks.
Further details and extracts of these and many
other beautiful books may be seen at

www.local-legend.co.uk

Lightning Source UK Ltd.
Milton Keynes UK
UKOW02f1256230215

246750UK00007B/191/P